Dying Out Here
Is Not An Option

PADDLEQUEST 1500

BOOK REVIEWS/TESTIMONIALS

Kevin Fedarko, Contributor, *Outside, Esquire, National Geographic Adventure, Time* and author of *The Emerald Mile*

"From the first page, Connelly puts you in the boat with him, feeling nature's rough edge; testing his mettle. The telling of his 1500 mile 75 day solo adventure at age sixty, with no ibuprofen, has highs and lows as well as laughs. Reading his account of 800 canoe and 700 kayak miles across such varying landscapes and seascapes is a grand adventure with many twists and turns. You will come away with appreciation and respect for our wild rivers, lakes, streams and oceans. Times of serenity and immense beauty to violent storms and high seas alone, dying out there was indeed possible many times. Glad he made it to tell the tale."

Richard Bangs, Contributor, *The New York Times, Slate, Huffington Post,* Host of PBS Richard Bangs' *Quests* and Richard Bangs' *Adventures with Purpose*

"*Dying Out Here Is Not An Option* is as wonderful a read as it is a wild ride. Connelly uses his luscious narrative style like a magic boat to transport readers effortlessly into his epic journey. With all the skills of an accomplished novelist, he vividly builds the universe he transects, detail by fascinating detail. You can feel the sun on your back and the cold water in your face as the struggle proceeds. It is a brilliant and engrossing tale of true grit and adventure, and the apotheosis that comes from an heroic effort. I'm so glad he survived to tell the shape of his waters."

Everett Potter, Contributor, Forbes.com, Editor, *Everett Potter's Travel Report*

"I read scattered dispatches of John Connelly's aquatic expedition on Facebook as it happened but now we have a full accounting of his remarkable voyage in both fresh and salt water. Amidst the rapids and tides, exertion and exhaustion, what jumps out is Connelly's incredible drive, a purpose matched by impressive physical prowess. He reveals himself to be a paddler's paddler in some of the most challenging waters of the Northeast. Let's face it, a single day of such kayaking or canoeing and dealing with the elements would be the stuff of a story that other paddlers would retell for the rest of their lives. Connelly had 75 such days in a row, an unbelievable daily roll call of challenges, discomfort and triumphs. Thank goodness for beer, cheeseburgers and an extraordinary assortment of friends who seemed to emerge from the woods to help when help was needed. Not to mention the unflagging support of his wife, Nicole. Read it as a diary of determination, even if your own paddling adventures are confined to the occasional afternoon in a canoe on a mill pond."

Will Goodall Copestake, Chilean Patagonia and Scotland
Sea Kayaking and Mountain Expeditioner, UK and Scotland Adventurer of the Year

"I first met John in Chilean Patagonia paddling the Rio Serrano river to explore icebergs and wilderness together for which I was his guide. With a characteristic understated modesty that seems to follow John both in person and his writing, he had put himself and his partner Nicole as 'intermediate' on our booking forms, although both were uttermost experts in their craft. We soon found a kinship amidst a shared passion of adventure, particularly that with a strong dose of type two fun. From a career of pioneering whitewater rafting and competitive paddling to a coffee magnate, seldom have I met such an inspirational couple as the Connellys. So when news of the PaddleQuest 1500 broke I followed with excitement, an ambitious goal which if anyone could achieve it would be John.

By dictionary definition an expedition is *"A journey undertaken by a group or person with a particular purpose, especially that of exploration, research or war."* Covering 75 days, two countries, four states, 22 streams and 58 lakes the Paddlequest 1500 covered it all. Johns exploration was route, his research his own boundaries and his war with the elements.

It is easy when writing an adventure book to focus on the 'epics' and of course for such an odyssey there are plenty to grip the reader to every page, but I find perhaps more special the attention John gives to the intricacies of daily expedition life. In a grand journey the quirks and quarrels of routine are the core reality of the experience and far harder to capture in writing. I found myself often drawn by the tale to my own experiences with a fond familiarity to what John was going through.

Although I have never visited most of his route I felt like I was right there with him, cheering on his trail angels, willing his next stroke to pass the wind and snow and relaxing to the call of the loon.

Dying Out Here Is Not An Option is more than just a tale of canoe and kayak adventures but an inspiring story of passion and devotion to the water, to the wilderness and to his wife Nicole. The end of a book is by no means the end of the adventure, and I am proud to have met John and to consider him a friend and look forward to following future Connelly classics."

Doug Welch, Executive Director, Maine Island Trail Association

"Few people can tell a story like John Connelly, and many fewer have stories to tell like this one! On tax day 2016—just after ice-out—John launched his canoe on a punishing 1,500-mile, 75-day paddling odyssey. The trip included the entire Northern Forest Canoe Trail, St. John River, Bay of Fundy, and Maine Island Trail. (Picture a lasso from upstate New York looping around the state of Maine.) Through his real-time tracking device, fans were able to follow his virtual rooster tail . . . and wonder anxiously every time the dot on the chart stopped moving, though it rarely stopped for long.

Dying Out Here Is Not an Option gets in John's head for 75 days of challenging on-water conditions and decisions —days of great inspiration and immense challenge even for an extraordinarily accomplished paddler. So pack your dry-bag and get ready!"

Karrie Thomas, Executive Director, Northern Forest Canoe Trail

"I found myself alternately rejoicing and commiserating with the pain and satisfaction of each hard fought trial and success, appreciating his descriptions of the skill required to pull off the endeavor and relating intimately with the sense of feeling at home in the watery outdoors. An inspiring adventure tale."

Dan Carr, Environmental Engineer, Adventurer and MITA board of trustees

"I really like books about real human powered journey's and have read a lot of them. I have spent many an evening reading accounts of hiking the AT, the PCT; or paddling around New Zealand, Scotland, Ireland, etc., and sailing around the globe. It is safe to say that I have read literally hundreds of books of this type and I have a closet full to prove it. I believe that John's story of his PaddleQuest 1500 trip has elements of some of the very best adventure writing. John's personal warmth, humor, and humanity come through quite well and makes this a compelling read. John is the real deal when it comes to adventure and his preparation for this trip was world class. His accounts of the kindness of strangers (aka trail angels), reverent appreciation of good meals, the apparent random encounters with friends and supporters in remote locations are wonderful reminders of the joy and appreciation for the little things that can be so special about human powered journeys.

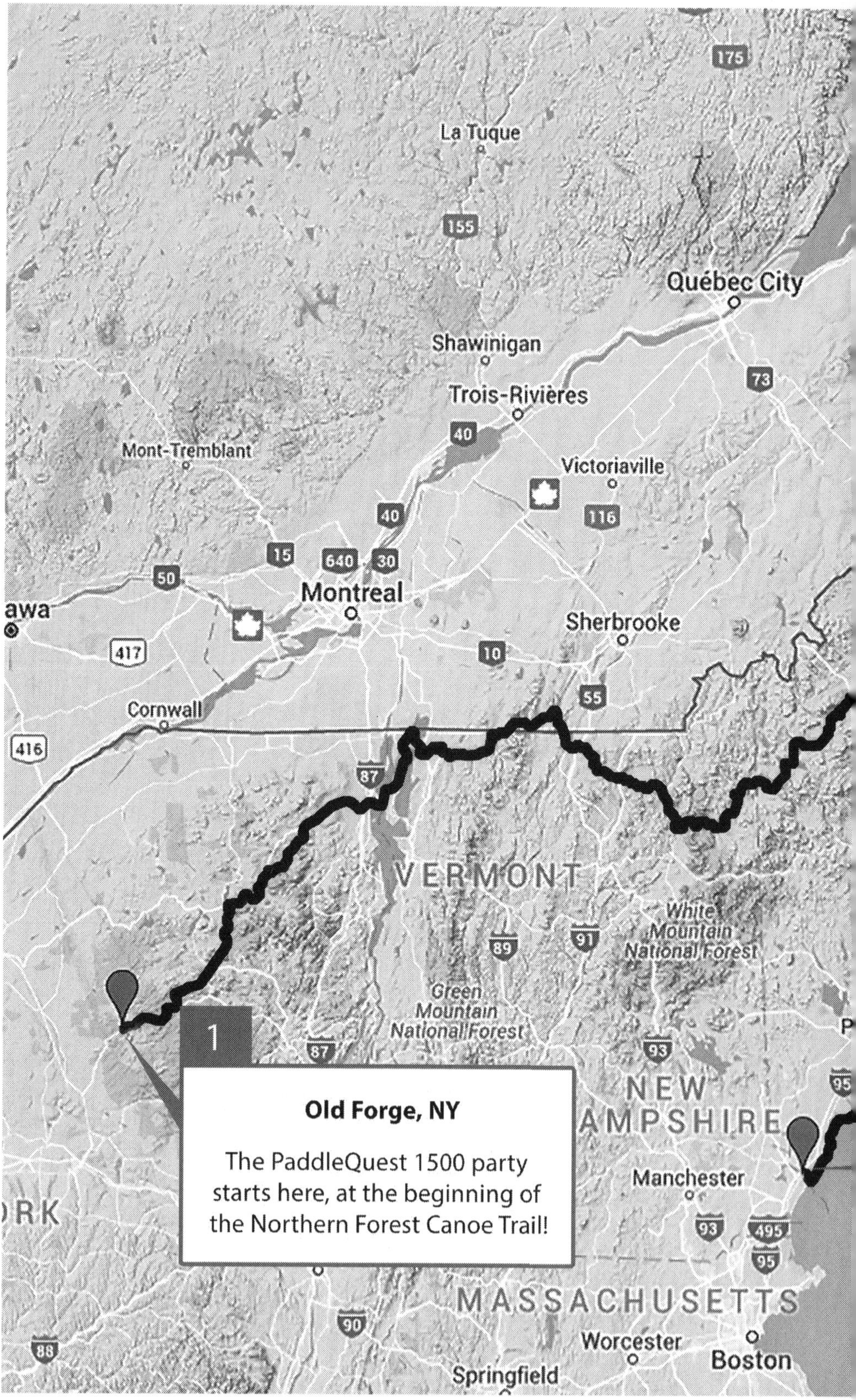
175
La Tuque
155
Québec City
Shawinigan
73
Trois-Rivières
40
Mont-Tremblant
Victoriaville
40
116
15
640
30
50
Montreal
awa
Sherbrooke
417
10
Cornwall
55
416
87
VERMONT
White Mountain National Forest
89
91
Green Mountain National Forest
87
93
NEW
AMPSHIRE
1
Old Forge, NY
The PaddleQuest 1500 party starts here, at the beginning of the Northern Forest Canoe Trail!
Manchester
ORK
93
495
95
MASSACHUSETTS
90
88
Worcester
Boston
Springfield

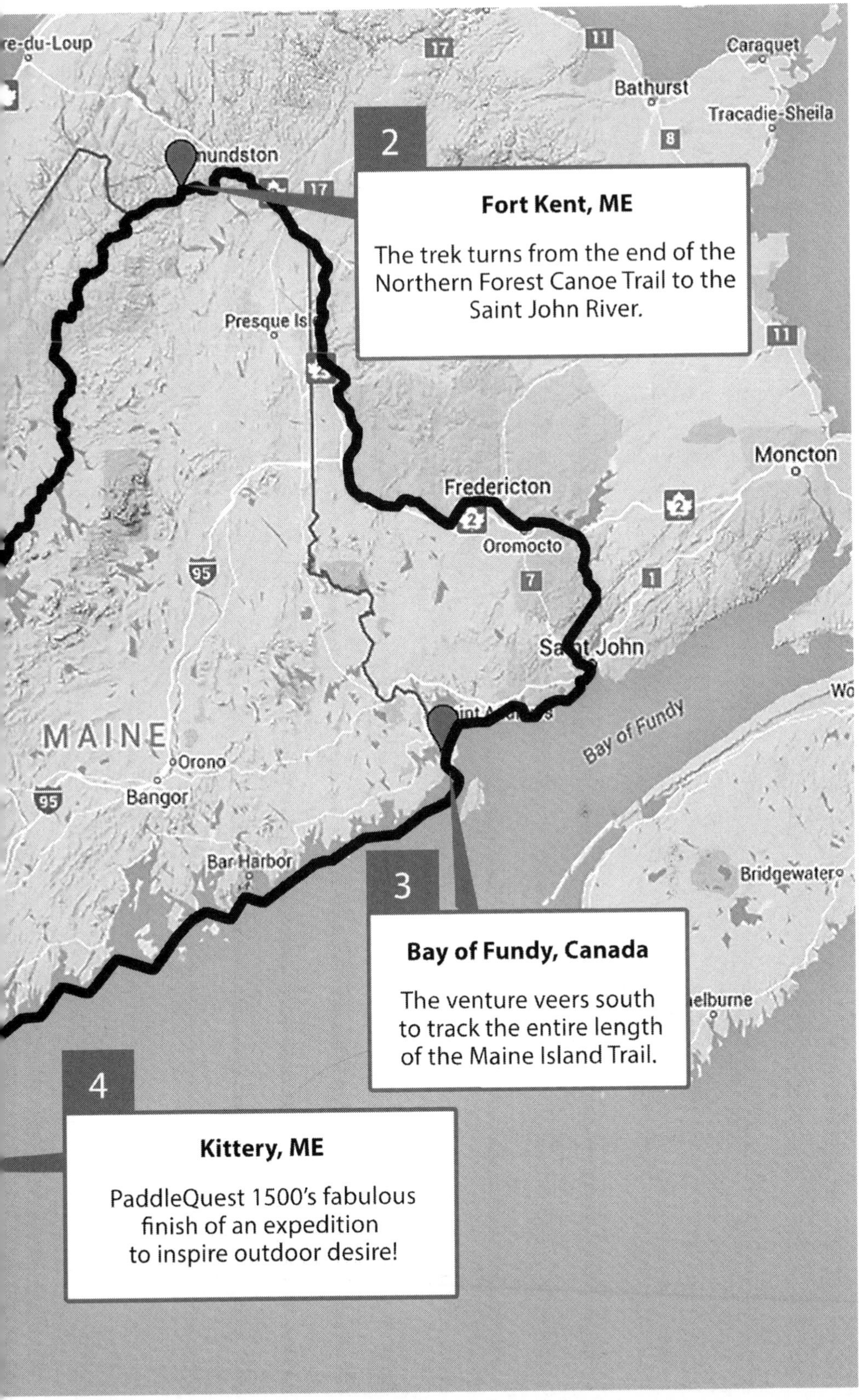

17
11
Caraquet
Bathurst
Tracadie-Sheila
8
2
17
Fort Kent, ME
The trek turns from the end of the Northern Forest Canoe Trail to the Saint John River.
11
Moncton
Fredericton
2
Oromocto
7
1
95
Saint John
Bay of Fundy
MAINE
Orono
Bangor
95
Bar Harbor
Bridgewater
3
Bay of Fundy, Canada
The venture veers south to track the entire length of the Maine Island Trail.
4
Kittery, ME
PaddleQuest 1500's fabulous finish of an expedition to inspire outdoor desire!

Dying Out Here Is Not An Option

PADDLEQUEST 1500

A 1500 Mile,
75 Day,
Solo Canoe &
Kayak Odyssey

by
John Connelly

ISBN: 978-0-692-15953-8

Library of Congress Control Number: 9780692159538

Published by
John Connelly
Yarmouth, Maine, USA
www.paddlequest1500.com

Produced by
Great Life Press
Rye, New Hampshire 03870
www.greatlifepress.com

A portion of the proceeds from the sale of this book benefit the Northern Forest Canoe Trail and Maine Island Trail Association.

For Nicole,
who unconditionally supports me
in even my boldest adventures
each and every day

Contents

Acknowledgments

There are many wonderful people who supported me and contributed to the success of my PaddleQuest 1500 expedition. First is my incredible wife, Nicole, without whose love and support, this never would have happened. Listing all of the ways SHE helped make this amazing adventure a reality is not possible.

My mom for being the earliest enabler and supporter of my passion for paddle sports without whom this, or for that matter anything else in my life, would not have been possible.

Northern Forest Canoe Trail for creating and maintaining the incredible 740-mile water trail, making the journey possible and supporting me on so many levels.

Maine Island Trail Association for creating and stewarding the nation's first water trail, and for supporting me in so many ways.

VisitMaine, Maine Office of Tourism, New Brunswick Tourism and Bay of Fundy Tourism for their support.

Bob Sehlinger for his support and coaching the efforts of an aspiring writer and teller of stories.

Bryn Keith for plowing through drafts and providing much needed feedback.

Falmouth Writers Group for valued feedback that helped me get it more right.

Huge debt of gratitude to Stu and Juli Haddon for editing this book and taking on my punctuation, and to Stu for helping me get it published.

So much thanks to everyone who so generously contributed to my GoFundMe campaign to make this expedition possible.

Thanks to my incredible sponsors:

Taja at Pulp & Wire for friendship and for supplying everything needed to create the PaddleQuest 1500 brand, including the website, blog and media management, and logos on the boats.

Fred at Shipyard Brewing Company for friendship and support on so many levels.

Dave at Stellar Kayaks for the best handling and lightest kayak that dealt with all the North Atlantic threw at it.

Mike and Jim at Wenonah Canoes for the best designed and lightest canoe for the job.

Werner Paddles for designing the best tools for the job.

Brian Threlkeld Photography for stunning images that tell a story.

Aaron at GrandyOats for the best breakfasts and snacks to keep me going.

David at Good To-Go foods for gourmet dehydrated meals I look forward to even now.

Adventurous Joe Coffee for an epic start to my days and to the team who made my leave of absence possible.

Mike at Hyperlite Mountain Gear for the best designed and manufactured gear to lighten my load.

Mark and Steve at NRS for the best paddling gear on the planet.

MSR for making it easy to manage water and fire every day.

Therm-A-Rest for making sleep something to look forward to.

Garmin for the InReach Explorer, making navigation a breeze and allowing me make good on my promise to Nicole to always be in touch and for her to know where I was.

Bangor Savings Bank for their support.

ReVision Energy for making it possible to use the sun to power my navigation and communication devices.

On the Water Trails:

Brian and Ned for joining me in the Adirondacks to make memories and to Brian for the amazing photos and Ned for helping to custom outfit my canoe.

To Peter, NFCT maintainer, for joining me on lake Champlain and sharing your knowledge.

Whit and Betsy for friendship, food and shelter on Lower Richardson Lake, ME.

Kevin and Doreen of Rangeley Region Lake Cruises & Kayaking in

Oquossoc, ME for opening a suite and giving me soup and cookies on a stormy, snowy night.

John, NFCT Maintainer, Stratton, ME for hospitality along the way.

Suzie, Russell, Rob and Greg at Northern Outdoors in The Forks, ME for the shuttles, cabin, and enabling me to guide a Dead River whitewater rafting trip on my way through.

John at The Birches Resort in Rockwood, ME for friendship, dinner and a cabin on the lake.

Liz and Al in Grand Isle, ME for saving me from that Armageddon-like storm with a roof, friendship and hot meal.

Dan for days of mostly gnarly paddling and making me laugh from Fredericton, NB to Machias, ME.

Adam and Rob for the laughs and guidance through the Saint John River's Reversing Falls.

Paul at Eco-Logical Adventures in Oromocto, NB for support.

Rafa from Rios Tropicales in Costa Rica for the surprise appearance in NB and the photos!

Ben, at Acadia's Oceanside Meadows Inn, for sleep, calories and friendship in Prospect Harbor, ME.

Ben and the Hurricane Island Foundation for warm hospitality in Penobscot Bay, ME.

David and Jane for friendship and the swank house on Orr's Island.

Fred at Shipyard Brewing Company and The Inn at Peaks for friendship and hooking me up with lodging, beer and food along the way.

John at The Colony Hotel in Kennebunkport for the wonderful hospitality.

Melissa and David for your hospitality on Cutt's Island and helping make the Finale Celebration on Fishing Island amazing.

The Maine Island Trail Association for support at the Finale and to Chris for accommodating my volunteer monitor skipper scheduling needs and for the photos.

CHAPTER ONE

— Inland Seas —

The raw wind whisking across the lake has abated, but has ushered in a steady, numbing drizzle; just enough to collect in the bottom of the canoe, sending each new drop rebounding on impact. My mind wanders back to cuddling my wife by the wood stove at home. I can smell birch smoke, dark roast coffee, and notes of herbs and citrus in her hair. I smile. Instead, here I am all alone on a wilderness Maine lake with a damp, penetrating chill in the air and rain falling. I wonder: what the heck was I thinking?

The canoe slides to a halt in sand and small stones at the base of tall pines. I heft my giant backpack, stow paddles into their clips inside the canoe, hoist the seventeen-and-a-half-foot boat onto my shoulders, and make for the dam. This is the day's first portage, and I make short work of it.

The lake teems with waterfowl preparing nests. Spring is near. The haunting cry of a solitary loon echoes over the static of rain peppering the lake's surface. As I round a point, revealing the expanse of open water ahead, a dozen geese honk into flight. Rain slows to a stop, and is replaced by a mist obscuring all but the nearest shore. From behind, a warmish wave of a breeze urges me forward, and pushes the mist off into stands of white pines that define the shoreline. I am reminded why I am here.

The forecast predicted the arrival of a cold front later in the day, and behind it, cooler air. There were no indications of a dynamic event. Right now there are no waves and a light breeze. Looking good. Instead of taking the much longer route that hugs the shoreline for wind protection, I'll take a direct heading across open water for my destination six miles distant. I should easily make it before the front rolls in. I pop a couple of chocolate-covered espresso beans and begin paddling with purpose.

I hear it before I see it. It's bearing down on me like a freight train. I'm really out there, a long way from shore, totally exposed. Damn. They were wrong. Seriously wrong. Suddenly, wind whips surface water sideways, even before the first wave is formed. Half-blinded, I dip the bill of my cap. At thirty-five miles per hour, droplets sting my face like pellets from a shotgun. The temperature plummets, and liquid morphs into sleet. In less than five minutes the calm surface has erupted into three-foot, white-capped waves that threaten to sink my loaded canoe. There are still four miles of open lake left to go. The snow begins.

"Best vacation ever," I say aloud, and vow that my next expedition will be in the tropics.

Dropping to my knees to secure the thigh straps that connect me to the boat for more control is not an option. I remain perched on my seat, feet jammed forward against the braces, knees spread, wedged beneath the thin edges of gunwale—the railing atop the canoe's sides. The waves are growing. Now, when I bottom out in the troughs, my surroundings disappear from view.

The nearest shelter is two miles away, straight into the gale. Maybe I can get there. I point the canoe slightly into the wind, and a gallon of forty-two-degree water dumps over the rail, adding eight sloshing pounds to the load. Damn. No short way to safety. I have to maintain course toward the far end of the lake, fully exposed to the onslaught for the duration. The slightest correction strokes slow my progress. I need strong, deliberate strokes to maintain direction and speed. I have to get through this nightmare.

Like the back of an angry hand, a rogue gust slaps frigid water against the side of my head, testing the neck gasket on my drysuit and my resolve to stay upright. I have to keep my cool. I can't get scared. My body will stiffen, strokes turning tentative and choppy, torso rigid, hips not moving with the boat's pitching and rolling over the waves. I'll get tippy and maybe flip over. A death grip on the paddle will only lead to fatigue and to losing my grip completely. If one little thing goes wrong, I can deal with it. If two things go wrong, I'm not so sure. That first little thing simply can't be allowed to happen. Deep breaths. Head up. Get into the flow of it. Become one with the water and the elements. Be fluid.

I call on forty-two years of Class V whitewater and surf-paddling experience, and a calm washes over me. The muscles in my jaw relax, I unclench my teeth and tell myself aloud, "You've got this."

This wins as the longest four miles of my life. I have to hip the boat away from breaking waves to keep from filling up, and paddle hard on only my upwind side. It is physically punishing. I can feel veins bulging; every muscle is pumped. I ignore my body's protest. Stay focused. Visualize success. Getting this done is a given and screwing it up is not an option. *Canoeist drowns in icy remote Maine lake in deadly storm.* This is not the kind of publicity I want for this expedition, and my wife will kill me if I die out here.

CHAPTER TWO

— The Making of the Thing —

As if it were their last meal, chickadees assault the bird feeder that hangs from the white oak's outstretched arm, while under the summer sun I sizzle like a slab of country bacon. I'll be logging weeks on the back deck of our Southern Maine home. I can eat BLTs, but I'm not allowed to do them. I have orders not to do any bending, lifting or twisting. With the grape-sized chunk of misplaced disc removed, my spine surgery is an apparent success. The paralyzing sciatica pain down my right leg is gone. Now it's up to me to follow doctor's orders or risk messing it all up.

"Over the next four weeks," he said, "work up to walking a mile."

The day after I went under the knife, I comfortably walked half of that. I'll be up to four miles by the time I see my surgeon again.

It'll take uncharacteristic discipline for me not to test my new spine. However, if I'm good, I know that after a few weeks of surfing the back deck, and with some careful rehab, I'll be back in action. I'm struck by how sobering it is, even alarming, to realize that I'm just one injury, or one ailment, away from not being able to do many of the things I want to do in life. I don't seem to be getting any younger, either, so as soon as I'm back in shape, there are some things that need to get done.

Getting old is like rusting. Oxidation does its insidious work in the background. I don't feel any different, but sometimes I look in the mirror and gasp at the image returning my stare. The paint has bubbled and the rust is showing through. It's just what happens.

2016 approaches and I'm about to hit the Big Six-Oh, but I don't feel like this chronological benchmark is any more significant than the others. I won't suddenly wake up finding myself in need of a bed pan just because I have turned sixty. It feels like a non-event to me.

Not so in the eyes of others, including my wife. They say turning sixty is a big deal and I need to do something special to celebrate. If it provides me with an excuse to do something special, I'm in it with both feet. The way I view it, I shouldn't just do something special. I should do something downright epic. But what will it be?

I was born a paddler. Although my parents didn't canoe or kayak, I must have received a recessive gene from some ancient branch of the family tree. It became the thing I did most naturally, so it takes no thought whatsoever to figure out what I should do.

Nobody has paddled both the Northern Forest Canoe Trail and the Maine Island Trail. I can paddle one and then the other. That's a first, and a big trip, but it's not epic. I've got it. How about I canoe the Northern Forest Canoe Trail from the New York Adirondacks in the west to its eastern terminus in Fort Kent, Maine; continue by kayak down the length of the Saint John River, through the Reversing Falls, down the Bay of Fundy; and then complete the Maine Island Trail to the New Hampshire border? That's a total of 1500 miles and should take around seventy-five days if all goes well. *That's* an epic adventure.

This expedition won't be only about fulfilling my personal ambitions. It will be about inspiring others to get off the couch and out from behind their screens; to get out there and enjoy the physical, mental and spiritual benefits to be realized by adventuring outdoors. *PaddleQuest 1500, an Expedition to Inspire Outdoor Desire* is born.

All my life, I have made conserving and stewarding our natural resources a priority. People only save what they love. Motivating more people to get out to enjoy these resources is my purpose, my life.

I started my guiding career as a whitewater rafting guide fresh out of high school in 1974. Much to my mother's chagrin, this jettisoned my anticipated course toward a law degree. Instead, I became an outfitter. In 1977 I founded my own company, operating in Maine, New York, West Virginia and Maryland, with sea kayaking operations in Maine,

North Carolina and Florida. In addition, I founded rafting operations in Switzerland and Italy.

After nineteen years, I sold the company, did safety and risk management work in the outdoors industry and then joined outdoors retailer L.L.Bean's management team, developing the L.L.Bean Outdoor Discovery Schools. Following a decade there, exposing many thousands to the outdoors, I continue to guide rafts and volunteer for the Maine Island Trail Association as a monitor skipper, stewarding island sites on Maine's coast.

One thousand five hundred miles over seventy-five days is a big deal. PaddleQuest1500 won't just be something fun or exciting, but something that will be meaningful and will test my mettle. It will be a significant canoe and kayak expedition and conditions are guaranteed to be difficult at times. I've heard tales of terror about big lakes and the North Atlantic Ocean blowing up unexpectedly, and people, many experienced, losing their lives. I've paddled in similar weather events, but with favorable outcomes—so far. No sugar coating, I know what I am getting into.

This expedition will have the distinction of being the first to link the Northern Forest Canoe Trail, Saint John River, Bay of Fundy and Maine Island Trail. One of my goals will be to garner increased support for the organizations that maintain these world-class water trails.

My awesome wife, Nicole, is the most supportive partner and spouse anyone could ever hope for. We met on a sea kayaking expedition on The Chesapeake Bay and we've paddled a lot of whitewater together. She knows what I'll be facing and has only two conditions for my proposed first-ever solo expedition. First is that every day she will know where I am and that I am safe. Second is that I'm not allowed to die. Fair enough.

I will start as early in spring as possible to catch high water flows in rivers and to be finished in time to enjoy the Maine summer with Nicole. It will start off cold and there will be storms. It's not going to be easy.

The journey will take me through two countries, four states, two provinces, twenty-two streams, fifty-four lakes and the North Atlantic Ocean. There will be 163 miles of upstream travel, and downstream there will be plenty of whitewater rapids to negotiate. Then there will be the frigid and notoriously tempestuous North Atlantic Ocean to paddle, alone, in a very small boat. I'll have much to do to make this thing happen and to make good on my promise.

I get my training started in earnest. At first, I need a bit of a nudge from Nicole. She wants me to train hard to make me bullet-proof so I will come back alive. I've always believed in training beyond the level of fitness required for merely accomplishing "the thing," whatever it is. I need to have reserved strength to deal with adversity, strain, injury, and unexpected events that require more of me in my most tired state. If I've got it, I survive. If I don't, I die. I ramp up my resistance and cardio training along with winter ocean paddling in both canoe and kayak, hitting the icy Maine coastal waters at least three days a week.

Setting out to organize sponsors, acquire gear and obtain funding is a full-time job. I still have my day job as co-founder, president and chief experience officer at Adventurous Joe Coffee LLC. So much to juggle, but not enough clowns.

Sponsors line up and funding is coming in. The reality hits home. I actually have to do this thing that I've been talking about for months. Be careful what you wish for.

Although I try to reassure her, Nicole begins to have second thoughts about the whole enterprise. It shakes her to the bone to think about the prospect of me alone, out in the wilds dealing with unknown dangers, and maybe never coming home. It concerns me as well, but call it faith, confidence, or whatever, I never doubt it. This may be a first-ever expedition, but I'm doing this thing, not attempting it. Or so I convince myself and tell everyone else.

When dealing with fears, the first step is to recognize and name them. Only then can they be put to rest. So we do. I am a professional risk manager, after all. I assure Nicole that I won't feel so pressed to get home that I'll take unreasonable risks. We pledge to rendezvous often during the trip so we can connect in person. A pinkie swear makes us both feel better. Underneath, we know that you just never know.

The next order of business is to make good on my promise to Nicole that she'll know my whereabouts. I need state-of-the-art satellite technology, so I court DeLorme, a Garmin brand, and innovator in GPS mapping technology. I manage to acquire their inReach Explorer for satellite navigation and communication. Linked with their Earthmate app, my iPad Air 2 and iPhone 6S, the inReach Explorer will allow me to communicate with Nicole anywhere, regardless of cell phone coverage. I'll have 160 characters per text and she can see where I am with real-time satellite tracking. I'll also have access to wilderness rescue services, should I run into an emergency that I am unable to manage on my own.

I'm not going to rely on the rescue button. Adventurers should be loathe to put rescuers at risk to save their own butts. If people are going to head into the wilds, they need to have the gear, knowledge, training and skills necessary for staying safe, and for self-rescue if they get into trouble. Calling 911 or calling in rescue by satellite should be an absolute last resort. I'm no exception.

That said, one of the benefits of being able to send and receive texts via satellite is that I would be able to communicate with rescuers about the nature of the emergency. This would allow them to muster the appropriate response and not throw all of their capabilities and resources my way if I don't need them.

With this technology, I may be in the middle of nowhere, but everyone, especially Nicole, will know exactly where I am. I'll have satellite tracking on the expedition website. People can watch my progress in realtime.

Later, I would learn that many people found that it was addictive to follow my blue line on the map. They became hooked on it. In some ways, it felt like the expedition version of "The Truman Show." With Nicole and all of my followers watching my progress and postings, I would be sharing the expedition with a supportive community. I'd never feel lonely. Alone, yes, but lonely, no.

An expedition is seldom truly unsupported. There is help with planning, logistics, supply drops and shipments. There are people poised to assist if you get into trouble, and those who wish for your success and safe return. There are also those who inspire you to take on something bigger than yourself, who prop you up and give you energy. If it weren't for loved ones, friends, sponsors and supporters of all kinds, an enterprise such as this would never get off the ground or be successfully executed. In my case, I owe much gratitude to many.

CHAPTER THREE

— First Strokes —

Finally. It is time to dip my paddle into the waters I've been dreaming about for years. No more training, no more plotting waypoints, sourcing gear, or talking about it. The time has come. The day is spectacular.

It is the morning of April 16th, 2016 in Old Forge, New York in the southwestern Adirondack Mountains. I sign in to the Northern Forest Canoe Trail Western Terminus logbook, and make official the start of my odyssey. I start to get excited, but a little trepidation taps me on the shoulder to keep things in perspective. This 740-mile canoe trail is merely the first leg of the larger journey.

Nicole joins me for the first day. I help launch her kayak from the sand beach, then put my Wenonah Voyager canoe into the first of the Fulton Chain Of Lakes. A perfect paddling day, not a breath of wind, and the temperature is already hitting sixty degrees. The water is springtime cold and the trees and grass are brown. The otherwise bustling tourist town is quiet this time of year, and there is an overall peacefulness about the day. Good vibes.

Seeing the canoe loaded with all I require to survive for the weeks to come, makes me think. This canoe and I are going to forge a relationship over the next eight hundred miles. What will that end up looking like? What will be the story?

The lakes are clear of ice. It's the second earliest ice-out in recorded history and the unusually warm winter has resulted in the complete absence of snowpack to feed spring rivers. If I don't get some rain, the sixty-three portages and carries, totaling fifty-four miles along the 740 miles of the Trail, will be increased significantly both in number and miles. I love paddling. But walking with a seventeen-and-a-half-foot canoe and sixty pounds of gear? Not so much. I need to get going and I'm going to need some help from above.

The weather is weird for this time of year, but I'll take it. It's an unseasonably glorious seventy degrees with no wind. Nicole paddles her kayak ahead of me, pulls out her camera, and lets me paddle by to snap a shot of my auspicious departure. Late morning, we stop at the village of Inlet to grab a sandwich at Kalil's Grocery and stretch our legs. We sit on the bank finishing our lunch and I'm conscious that I'm savoring every moment with her. We'll end the day on Racquette Lake, about twenty miles in all, including three portages. Today will give Nicole a real sense of the Trail as it knits together numerous watersheds over its length.

We pull our boats on their canoe carts over a winding trail through the woods, passing over the highest point of the Trail at just over 1800 feet. The day of portages, paddling across lakes and down meandering streams is bitter-sweet for both of us. Throughout, we look at each other and smile that knowing smile. The one where you're happy to be together, but know that time is ticking down to a parting that neither of you can bear.

People ask what the hardest part of the expedition was for me. It wasn't the seventy-two-hour intestinal bug that turned me inside-out and sapped my energy. It wasn't making over twenty miles a day including portages. It wasn't the freezing nights and mornings when all my paddling clothes and gear were frozen stiff as a board or using my body heat to thaw them. It wasn't the blackflies, so thick they'd clog my orifices and suffocate me if I weren't wearing a head net. It wasn't the violent storms throwing gawd-awful winds and waves my way, giving the words "cold front" chilling meaning. It wasn't the relentless days of paddling, despite small craft warnings, through eight-foot seas with wind swells driven by twenty-mile-per-hour headwinds and chaotic reflection waves bouncing off vertical granite cliffs and rocky coastlines.

It was embarking on an audacious and perilous journey without the love of my life.

The next morning, I strike out alone on a cloudless blue day with not so much as a wisp of breeze. I have a 1480-mile adventure ahead of me. I should be excited. Exhilarated. I am far from either.

Throughout the months of training and planning, Nicole kept reminding me that she was much too young to be a widow. I'd laugh uneasily, but she wouldn't even crack a smile. It isn't until now that the gravity of her message truly hits home.

I will never forget those first strokes, leaving her standing alone on the lake's sandy shore, blowing a kiss and waving her hand in the shimmering low-angle light of early morning. It's all I can do to paddle toward open water. My heart is breaking. I feel a sharp, deep pain I've never before experienced. So much unknown lies ahead, and yes, danger. I have to make good on my promise. I'm determined to end the expedition in better shape than when I started. My resolve: I can't let anything go wrong. Not one little thing.

It is early spring in the Adirondacks. Nothing is green, the water is forty-ish but feels colder. Although it has been an unusually warm winter and spring, I have the feeling that things will even out in the end. They usually do. I'm unlikely to dodge the bullet entirely and expect things to go south weather-wise at some point. Right now, I'm going to relish every moment.

My navigation shows that the next portage on the Racquette River is just ahead. It is around Buttermilk Falls, over unimproved trail. Most expedition paddlers carry their boat and gear on separate trips. I want to make one trip with my carries, to save time and walking distance. Now that plan is about to get tested. I won't be able to use the canoe cart so I'll have to carry that too; another ten awkward pounds. I pull ashore and steal a fleeting glimpse of the waterfall's entrance, hoping to see an obvious route for lowering the canoe by rope, but it only confirms the big white *Portage Here* sign on shore and the guidebook's description of a mandatory carry.

I strap everything I can to my pack, and tie the rest in the canoe. The ungainly pack requires me to sit on the ground to get it on. Arms wave wildly, and reach for handholds in thin air. I try to get my feet under the load, but find myself back in the starting position. I scoot over a couple of yards and pull myself vertical using a nearby birch, like a bear moving up a tree in a series of ascending hugs. I'm laughing out loud at myself and glad there are no bystanders. I waddle to the boat, bend my knees to reach down and hoist it over my head. It's up, but teeters and sways, almost too far. Surely, I will get better at this.

For the first time on the trip I realize I need to edit my gear to make the load more manageable. The pack, with everything hanging from it, feels like something north of seventy pounds, and the canoe with spare paddles and such, another thirty-six or so. I feel my arches flattening. I lost thirty-two pounds over the winter on the Fast Metabolism Diet. My empty canoe weighs thirty-two pounds. Hell, I lost a canoe. Somehow my arches feel better.

I put in below the ten-foot falls and see two relatively clean lines for a whitewater kayak. Maybe another day. Emerging from the Class II rapids below, I enter Long Lake in glorious seventy-three-degree weather with boundless sunshine; not a cloud to be seen and not even a ripple; just two brook trout slurping olive mayflies from the mirrored surface. It appears as if they are kissing the sky.

Later in the day I join two of my best friends from Maine at a lakeside motel. Brian Threlkeld, an accomplished outdoor adventure photographer, and Ned Merrick, a talented craftsman, woodworker and outdoorsman. Both tall, handsome men possess mad outdoor skills and both are the type of human beings you crave spending time with if you like intelligent conversation and laughter. The next four days on the water with them in their tandem Wenonah Adirondack canoe will be a treat. I'm glad to have company on the Saranac Lakes and part of the Saranac River that includes portages and rollicking stretches of white-water. Over beers and dinner at a tavern we discuss the days ahead, go over their final checklists and agree to get on the water early, to start putting the Saranac Lakes behind us and reach the river of the same name, where the action lies.

It's good to have company when paddling unfamiliar waters, although sometimes things don't go according to plan. Our lake travel goes smoothly, but the trouble starts on the river as we enter Trail Rapid. It's the second of three busy Class II sections, roughly forty miles before reaching Plattsburgh, New York, and Lake Champlain. I'm comfortable reading the rapids as I go, leading our flotilla of two. Fifty yards into the second set, I look back over my right shoulder to make sure the separation between boats is ample, but close enough to allow the duo to see my route. Unlike the other times I've checked on them, Brian and Ned now appear as two heads next to their overturned canoe, bobbing through choppy waves and current funneled between granite boulders. I have to get to them quickly, contain the situation, and take them and their gear-laden boat safely to shore before the cold water seriously affects them.

I need to paddle to shore, pull up my boat, and run upstream with my rescue rope to help them. Back-paddling furiously, I ferry into a midstream eddy behind a flat, black boulder the size of a coffee table. *Damn, this boat is long and not very nimble with all of this gear. Not made to spin on a dime. Must get pointed more upstream.* I back out of the far side of the eddy, allowing the downstream current to grab the stern and begin the pivot toward the right river bank.

I pull hard, sweeping strokes on the downstream side, and drive forward into the oncoming current. The bow is pushed more downstream than I'd like. I make an arcing turn toward shore but am driven downstream slightly sideways. I see a jagged rock just beneath the surface. It's unavoidable. I wince as the boat scrapes over it loudly. *That'll leave a mark.*

The shoreline is boulder-strewn with brush and low-hanging tree branches. I pull the canoe halfway out of the river, grab a rescue throw-bag containing sixty feet of rope, and bolt upstream as best I can amid the chaos of slippery rock and moss.

My friends have managed to stop their downstream progress by hanging onto rocks with one hand and holding the capsized canoe in slow current with the other. Looking like drowned rats, they're laughing about their little mishap. They're obviously unhurt, so we focus on lining the canoe to shore, dumping the water out of it, and getting them underway as soon as possible.

I help them get situated and launched back into the rapids. They're soaked and clearly chilled; paddling will do them good.

Time to return to the canoe and inspect the hull. I roll it onto its side and the damage is clear. The rock has sliced almost all the way through two layers of kevlar. It has to be repaired, properly.

My buds are leaving tomorrow. The forecast is for cool temps and a chance of rain, tonight and for the next day or so. Definitely not suitable weather for a proper fiberglass repair to the wounded canoe. It's decided that Brian and Ned should hitch a ride to retrieve Brian's car where he left it two towns downstream. The plan is to car-top the canoe to Plattsburgh where we can perform a fiberglass repair in the hallway of a hotel.

As we wheel our boats down the Silver Lake road toward Clayburg, the spokes on one of my wheels disintegrate so I fall behind Brian and Ned to repair it. They get picked up by a couple of good ole boys in a pickup truck. A young girl is driving; a phone book would have been useful to help her see over the steering wheel. The girl is behind the wheel because the men are too drunk to drive.

The grandfather says to Brian, "Don't worry, she may have failed her driving test this morning, but she's doing a good job!"

Brian and Ned tell the men about the expedition, the necessity of repairing the canoe, and thus the need to retrieve Brian's car. The father, "road soda" in hand, offers to take them to get the car and extends an invitation to join in on the family's backyard picnic dinner. First, they reverse direction and pull up to me on the side of the road where I'm fashioning spoke reinforcements out of whittled branches, secured in place with Gorilla Tape. They tell me which house is theirs and that it's only a half mile further on.

"Just ask for Linda," they say. "Tell her that you've arrived for the cookout!"

The generosity of these people is outstanding. They drive Brian to get his car. Then we all sit down at folding tables on the lawn to enjoy a down-home meal of steak on the grill and a medley of garden vegetables in casserole dishes. After dessert, one of the girls is thrilled to show off her giant pet lizard. It's obvious they don't have visitors like us often. Three generations of family are living in adjacent houses backed by acres of farmland. They make us feel right at home. A delightful slice of Americana. My first "Trail Angels."

Grateful for their warm hospitality, we hate to eat and run, but that's exactly what we do. We have to get a room, dry out and fix the boat. Our new friends let us keep our gear and one canoe behind their house. I know exactly where we need to stay.

We head to the Comfort Inn in Plattsburgh where there's a brew pub and a water park. Yes, an indoor water park with a huge twisting slide ejecting its contents into an eighty-degree pool. After storing the canoe indoors, we grab our shorts and jump right in to do laps around and down the slide. I hadn't anticipated this being part of my Northern Forest Canoe Trail experience, but it sure works.

Ned dons latex gloves and kneels next to the canoe to perform the fix. As epoxy fumes waft down the hallway, a hotel guest passes by, cocks her head, and says, "You don't see this everyday."

Boy, is she right. We add an extra drop of catalyst to the mix to accelerate the curing process, cover the patch with plastic for a smooth, hydrodynamic finish, and head to the brew pub down the hall.

With the canoe successfully repaired, my friends drop me at the point where we left off yesterday. For them, it's back home to Maine. As they escort me to the put-in on the river, I'm taken completely off guard by unexpected waves of emotion. In the moment, I am mindful that I'm going to be alone, with no guarantees of seeing them, or anyone else I know, ever again. Brian holds out his iPhone and takes an "ussie" of the three of us. From that moment, until I paddle away, I can't make eye contact or speak to them. If I try, I'll let what is so near the surface spill out and that's not the way I want to leave them. I'll never forget what they say as I paddle away: "You're doing something way bigger than yourself, man. And that's awesome."

CHAPTER FOUR

— Low Point —

In mid-afternoon, everything turns to crap. Literally. The weather. And me. Since leaving those guys, I've been feeling drained of energy, with loose bowels and a sense of urgency turning to desperation. It reminds me of the six bouts I had with a waterborne parasite called *giardia*. "Beaver Fever" they call it. Symptoms include explosive diarrhea (I think that may be the medical term), lethargy, and feeling like death would be welcome if it were to come sooner rather than later. Not the best for paddling. Especially sealed into a drysuit.

(Comparing notes days later, Ned and I concluded that we got into some tainted food that night. I turned inside out for the next seventy-two hours and Ned heaved his way back to Maine. This required Brian to pull over six times to eject poor Ned, and then Ned to eject whatever it was in his gut. We thought it was the pub food because Brian didn't eat there and he was totally fine. When passing through on business, I had eaten at that same pub a couple of times without incident. After this, I think I'll stick to drinking the beer.)

As I part company with Brian and Ned, the weather is stellar but I am not. I feel lousy. I'm wearing my dry bibs over NRS HydroSkin pants but go lighter up top with a rash guard, short-sleeved HydroSkin top and short-sleeved paddling jacket. A front is due to move through in mid-afternoon, but it's not supposed to be severe at all. I'm just under five miles away from my day's end campsite when I notice slate gray clouds looming over the mountains to my left. These are angry clouds and not indicative of a subtle change in weather.

The next thing I know, there are rear-quartering whitecaps on the river and I'm fighting to keep the canoe heading downstream. The rain doesn't start with a sprinkle; it pours hard in wind-whipped sheets and a gust forces my ball cap loose. I take my hand off the paddle long enough to cram the hat firmly on my skull. In that brief instant, the canoe spins into the wind. It's a struggle to recover the boat angle before I'm turned around completely. Timed with the unweighting of the bow when lifted by waves, I employ strong, arcing, forward sweeps and stern draw strokes, that put me back on track. A U-shaped waterfall forms off the brim of my ball cap. I'm drenched and the temperature drops ten degrees into the mid-forties.

I want this to be over. I only have another hour or so to go, so I decide not to pull over to dig out an insulation layer and wiggle into my dry top. I don't want to prolong being out here, and soon enough, I'll be done for the day. A rationalization by an irrational person. Later, I'll attribute this poor decision to my depleted state from being ill. That's no excuse. I know better and should have pulled over to layer up. By the time I hit the day's take-out, I'm in stage one hypothermia: my teeth are chattering and I'm shaking uncontrollably, like dry leaves in a stiff autumn breeze.

It takes longer than I hoped, but I'm finally at the Cadyville town beach take-out. I'm tempted to put up my shelter right here and crawl in, but it's in full view of the road. Probably not safe. I have to stop losing body heat. The rain now mixes with sleet. I try opening my pack, but the fingers aren't doing what the brain is ordering. Now I'm verbally ordering my fingers to work. With deliberate effort, I pull out an expedition-weight shirt and weatherproof dry top. With my back to the wind, I hold them to my chest, attempting to keep them dry. I'm changing in rain, sleet and wind but neither cold nor wet register in my brain. My fingers remain uncooperative and now the shirt is pissing me off. It's sticking to my wet skin and it's taking forever to put it on. I'm startled by the size of my goosebumps.

A jacked-up black Dodge Ram pick-up truck with brush guard, winch, and oversized wheels backs into a parking spot further up the beach. A lone woman in her twenties sits at the wheel. Hip-hop bass reverberations telegraph through the ground. As I struggle to pull on my dry top, she opens the front passenger window. I hear 2Pac's *Hit 'Em Up*, clearly now. Out flies an empty fifth of booze. Rear tires kick up wet sand and off she drives.

Reaching deep, I force myself to gather my pack, put the canoe on its wheels and head up to the road. I need shelter and warmth, fast. I go directly to the first house to ask if there is any local lodging within walking distance. Little do I know, but I'm about to have the worst human contact on the entire 1500-mile trip.

The paint is mostly peeled and the loose siding boards could use attention with a hammer. The small, single-level house with attached, doorless garage sits only a few yards from the busy road, and the rust-riddled car in the yard probably wouldn't pass a DMV inspection. These should be my first warning signs, but I am addled from the hypothermia. Two full minutes after my first knock, a stocky, unshaven figure in a formerly white wife-beater shirt, cracks open the door and peers out. He says nothing, but motions to the open garage. With effort, I meet him there. Everything is taking effort now. Even standing up.

Through clattering teeth, I explain what I am doing and inquire about local lodging. I sound like talking castanets.

He laughs and says, "You're in Cadyville, man. There's nothin' here."

"Any campgrounds?" I ask.

He shakes his square, balding head. Deflated, I ask if anyone would object to my camping on the town beach. Now it's just about dark, so I'm not as concerned about being visible from the road. My biggest risk might be getting hit by a flying booze bottle. The rain is easing somewhat.

"You don't need to camp on the beach. You can camp in my yard. And you can use my bathroom to take a shower, too," he drawls.

I can't believe my good fortune. How lucky. Lucky? Hell, the way I'm feeling, I've just been *saved.*

"Your name again?" I ask.

"Mike," he says.

In staccato bursts, I manage to clatter out, "Thank you so much, Mike. You're a savior."

I mean it from the bottom of my heart. I gratefully accept his offers, then the bombs start dropping.

"You probably should know that there's a woman living with me that is a bad alcoholic. She drinks way too much. She gets violent. But she should pass out early and then you can come in," he says nervously. "And she has a dog."

Uh oh. A dog. As wiped-out as I am, this certainly wakes me up.

"It's bitten a few people and it's meaner than she is."

I ask how he is going to keep the dog from attacking me after the woman goes to sleep.

His eyes roll toward the floor, he shrugs his hairy shoulders and says, "I have no idea."

Well, that's enough for me. I ask if I can just sit on a chair in his garage long enough to gather myself to set up my tent. I add that I have no intention of entering his house or using the bathroom with the dog in there, and that I'll leave at first light to get back on the river. He nods, slowly turns away and slinks back inside. I am circling the drain. I know I should eat, but the thought nauseates me. I melt into a moldy, overstuffed chair and pass out.

Less than ten minutes after Mike leaves me in the garage, the door to the house abruptly swings open. I can do nothing more than open one eye. Before me stands a woman in tattered gray sweat pants and sweat shirt with wild black hair that, no kidding, is standing straight on end. She takes up the entire doorway: a rectangular dark figure with no light behind to create an outline. She starts yelling at me as she wobbles down the four or five steps into the garage. Both eyes now open, I'm slumped in the chair trying to comprehend what I am witnessing. Now she's bent over me, yelling in my face. The acrid odor of turpentine fills my nostrils. I realize it's her breath which confirms that I'm not hallucinating after all.

"I don't know you! I don't know you!" she yells over and over again, glazed red eyes smoldering in their sockets. "You will never step foot in my house! I have a dog I will sic on you. He'll tear you up! He'll tear up all those expensive clothes you're wearing and make you bleed!"

I try to interrupt to apologize for being an inconvenience and to tell her my story and introduce myself. I realize immediately that it's futile. So I sit in the chair and take it, hoping she won't strike out at me with those clenched, troll-like fists she's waving about. Her venom spent, she turns on the heel of her slipper; heaves her way back up the stairs; throws open the door and, with a slam, she's gone.

Holding my head in my hands, I try to figure out if the incident really happened. It's dark out. I'm overdue for calling Nicole. I have two bars on my phone. I go to Favorites and touch her name. I need to talk to someone who loves me. She answers on the first ring. She was watching my tracking line on the computer and saw that I was off the river and hadn't moved for a while. I let her know that I'm okay and that I'm camping in someone's yard in Cadyville, New York. I try my best to sound normal but she sees through it.

I don't want her to worry about me, but at the same time I could use some support right now. So I tell her about my condition and what's going on, but neglect to mention my psycho hosts, to alleviate undue worry. Attempting to reassure her that I'll be fine, I tell her that I'll set up my tent after a few minutes of rest. I must sound like crap. I'll bet she's not buying it. After virtual long-distance hugs, we say goodbye for now.

Vibrations. Giant crickets chirping. One eye snaps open, the other remains closed. I look at the phone in my hand as if it's the enemy. I see Nicole's name on the screen. Looking at the time, I hit the green button, realize I haven't moved and an hour has elapsed. Somehow she knows I fell back asleep. She puts me on notice that I need to get up from the chair right now, put up my tent and sleep. I agree, and we hang up after I promise to update her in the morning.

The 40-watt bulb overhead casts a pall over the interior of the garage and my now-standing shadow stretches onto the gravel driveway. I contemplate the idea of skipping the tent and pulling out the sleeping bag and pad to sleep on the floor. Not an option. Too cluttered and utterly filthy. Oh yeah, and then there's that dog.

Between the persistent bad weather and my condition, it's a world-class lousy night. I keep wondering when that crazy woman is going to let Cujo out to do his business. All I have between me and two rows of frothing fangs is a single layer of Dyneema Composite tent material.

I must not sleep in. I have to leave before she lets that dog out in the morning.

Sleeping too late isn't an option. My roiling intestines insist that I dash from the tent into the cold drizzle every twenty or so minutes.

My usual practice, my Leave No Trace responsible outdoorsman practice, is out the window. These are dire times. These are emergencies. Normally, I would use my Wag Bags for solid waste. Carry in, carry out. The Wag Bag system includes two degradable bags, one for poo and the other for carrying your prize with you for proper disposal. There's a powdery gelling and deodorizing agent in the poo bag that solidifies the stuff and makes it biologically inert, so you can chuck it in a trash can and don't have to find a place that accepts human waste. The only hitch is that you can't pee in the bag. Well you can, but why haul that around with you, too? To pull off the separation, you have to develop a technique. In time, you get used to it. Tonight, under these extreme circumstances, I'm not standing on ceremony. I'm "lettin' 'er fly" behind Mike's shrubs.

Morning approaches. It's pitch black and the sun hasn't even thought about making an appearance. I pack up by headlamp, make one last urgent purge in nearby bushes and get on the river. The dank morning darkness is a metaphor for my situation and for my frame of mind. I'm dehydrated and still haven't eaten. And I don't want to.

Relieved to have that nightmare in the rearview mirror, I paddle on. Drizzle has deteriorated into a mist that has now cleared. The canoe has been applying its signature to the morning's glassy waters for twenty minutes. A cool upstream breeze evaporates the beads of sweat on my face, making me shiver. I'm running on fumes. It's time to eat something, anything. Drifting downstream, I unwrap a chocolate fudge Clif Bar. If I can stomach anything, it'd have to be chocolate. When can I not eat chocolate?

I take a sip of water. Halfway through my bar . . . *Oh no.* I shove the other half into the pocket of my life jacket, grab the paddle and stroke to shore like I'm being chased. I yank the boat clear of the water, reach into the deck bag and grab a roll of toilet paper. Scurrying into the woods, I frantically tug at my dry top. As I peel it over my head, I almost pull out all my hair with the sticky neck gasket. I slip off the shoulder straps of the dry bibs and yank them and the pants to my ankles. I back almost too far over a log, catch myself before going turtle and experience yet another explosive event. A near miss. Best vacation ever.

This process would repeat itself for three days with varying degrees of success. Paddle like hell. Grab the TP. Dive into the woods. Repeat. My choices are to hunker down in my tent feeling sorry for myself until I feel better, which could take who knows how long, or just suck it up and get better while putting more miles behind me. So instead of throwing myself a pity party, I press on with two rolls of TP, hoping for the best. It takes every ounce of energy I have to stay on track, paddling twenty-plus miles with as many as four portages a day. I do manage to nibble a snack here and there and sip water, but I'm running a growing deficit.

I think about Nicole at home, my friends, my ninety-three-year-old mother in Maryland, all fretting about me. Right now, nobody is more concerned about me than I am. I wonder when the misery will end; when I'll eat a meal again or have energy to do more than barely function. I just want to pull ashore and assume the fetal position until this is over. I work hard to envision the day when I'm not worried about soiling myself; when I'll be able to appreciate what I'm doing out here. I don't even notice things like the cotton clouds floating across a blue sky or the tree-lined corridor winding through the woods or deer bounding from the shore as they sense my approach down the rapids. I hear them, but I don't bother turning my head to look.

At dusk, I paddle the small rapids through the city of Plattsburgh, New York into the mouth of the Saranac River. Unfolded before me is the expanse of Lake Champlain where the stories of high seas and mayhem seem preposterous given its current chilly calm in the fading light. I quietly land amongst fly fishermen angling for salmon at the city's boat ramp.

Pulling the canoe up on shore, I once more have an experience unique to being the season's first Northern Forest Canoe Trail through-paddler. There's no log book in place yet to sign at the NFCT kiosk; to register my name to show I've made it this far; to leave a message for those who follow. In my weakened condition, I feel sad about it, while at the same time realizing that this reaction is completely ludicrous. I'm not quite right.

Ten minutes of not paddling allows the cold to set in. Trying unsuccessfully to get in front of the shivers, I put on a warm layer and call Nicole. I need to get a warm, dry roof over my head with accommodation that stretches to a flush toilet and a closet full of TP. Within ten minutes she has a room reserved at a lakeside motel about a mile-and-a-half paddle up the lake. Grateful is a woefully inadequate expression.

I scour the area and find a portable toilet at a construction site half a block away, then get back on the water. I land the canoe on the Caribbean-like white sand beach of the Golden Gate Motel, pull the boat up a couple of yards and walk toward the office. A bright-faced man with a spring in his step is heading my way.

"Are you John Connelly?" he calls out, making me laugh. "Your wife, Nicole, said you'd be coming. Let me show you to your room."

Little does he know that the next morning his housekeeping staff will have one of its worst days.

For the first time in two days I feel like I probably want to eat something. I call for a pizza delivery and try to rehydrate as best I can. The sight of fluids and the thought of food are still repulsive, but I'm a bit better and I need to eat. I'm losing weight and starting to resemble a corpse.

The knock at the door prompts my quickest reaction in days. I grab the food, settle the bill and flop into bed with the box. My stomach doesn't mirror my brain's enthusiasm. I can only choke down two slices. It'll be cold pizza for breakfast.

Pushing the box to the other side of the bed, I draw my knees to my chest and pass out without turning off the light. Like the previous night, whenever I relax in my sleep, *everything* relaxes. I manage it with varying degrees of success so I don't sleep much. I wouldn't wish this intestinal bug on my worst enemy. Well, come to think of it, there's one who might deserve it. But only for forty-eight hours, certainly not seventy-two.

My friend, Peter, an experienced paddler and resident of the Vermont side of Lake Champlain, has offered to make the crossing with me from New York to the Vermont Islands. When local knowledge is available, I like to take advantage of it. He is an affable man who paddles a wooden canoe he designed and built, and strokes with a paddle he handcrafted. He has through-paddled the Trail and joins others for a section of Lake Champlain when he can. I'll see him in the morning. Before his arrival, I need to grab a taxi and get to a pharmacy for diarrhea medication.

At 7:00 am I nibble away at two slices of cold pizza, refill the hydration pack on my life jacket, and organize lunch and snacks for the day. It's the same lunch and snacks I've packed the previous two days but haven't eaten. I hope that today will be different. Fingers crossed.

I'm already dressed for the water when the cab arrives. I climb in, wearing a life jacket over my drysuit, clutching a waterproof bag.

"Take me to the nearest pharmacy for Imodium AD," I say.

The driver is Asian-American, well-dressed and more cheerful than I am this early in the morning. His eyes in the rearview examining the oddity in the back seat are clearly saying, *You're too early for Halloween, so what's your deal?* So, I tell him my story. He's intrigued and says he admires people who follow their dreams and take on big challenges. He likes to canoe, but can't fathom what I'm doing.

The cab stops at the Condo Pharmacy a mile down the road. I ask the driver to wait while I make my purchase. A few short minutes later, I climb back in, rip open the packaging and flush the pills down my gullet with water from the hydration pack. I can't wait to be on the mend.

We arrive back at the motel and he tells me how much the fare is. I pull a credit card out of the dry bag, which prompts a laugh.

"Dude, this is Plattsburgh. No credit cards here. You've gotta pay cash."

I don't have this much cash on me. I ask him to wait while I excavate some greenbacks from the dry bag in the canoe.

He laughs again and says, with the warmest eyes I think I've ever seen on a man, "Friend, it's your lucky day. I don't want to take your money. It'd be bad karma. You just feel better soon and I wish you good luck on your amazing journey."

With that, he reaches out, shakes my hand and pulls away. What a contrast with the intoxicated She-Beast and her canine enforcer I left upstream.

Ah, a text from Peter saying he's almost reached the motel. I spot a speck on the water moving slowly my way, less than a half-mile out. I hit the head one last time and make the finishing preparations. I'm ready to go when he arrives. Lake Champlain is like glass as we strike out for the crossing. Peter has a wealth of knowledge about Champlain history and canoe building. He is terrific company. We chat all the way to the ferry terminal on Cumberland Head where I scurry to the restroom. I hurry more out of habit than from actual need. It dawns on me that things are already better. I pledge out loud never to go anywhere without Imodium AD, ever again.

We stop at Hero's Welcome, a convenience store and restaurant on North Hero Island, Vermont. This is where I say goodbye to Peter and eat my first complete meal in three days. It is a generous smoked turkey and Swiss cheese sandwich on wheat with lettuce, tomato, mayo, and a dill pickle on the side, rounded off with a big fat fudge brownie for dessert. Unforgettable. I'm back.

After a few more miles of glassy water, paddling up Lake Champlain takes me to North Hero Island State Park, which is not yet open. The sky is clear and cold, as the orange ball of flame melts over the serrated horizon. The jagged silhouette gives me a sense of the distance traveled. It is surreal to think that I have come from the far side of those distant Adirondack Mountains.

I scope out the park beach, and pitch my shelter on the leeward side of a locked bathroom on the waterfront. I would be sheltered from wind off the lake and exposed to the morning rays of sunrise, which should provide some early warmth while I make coffee and breakfast. I'm able to hang my wet stuff in the bathroom's roofed entryway to drip. I know it won't dry, and will freeze solid overnight, but at least it won't be as heavy.

The sun's final curtain call leaves cold air falling all around like a damp blanket. Grateful to devour an actual dinner, I put dishes away and crawl into the sleeping bag, pulling the hood over my head. Hunkered down in this cocoon, I scroll through the series of journal posts on my phone and add one for today. What a day it has been. No intestinal emergencies and I'm feeling almost normal. Hurray.

I am unable to fall asleep, and lie listening to the lake gently lapping the shore. I feel alone. Very alone. There's no cell service, so Nicole and I trade text messages on the inReach Explorer. I'm missing her terribly. I haven't seen her since Day Two and won't see her again until Newport, Vermont, after I ascend the Missisquoi River into Quebec, cross the Grand Portage and paddle back into Vermont to the south end of Lake Memphremagog. The longest we've been apart was the ten days she was in Morocco on business. Today makes thirteen days apart.

I think back to our meeting on a sea kayaking expedition twelve miles offshore on The Chesapeake Bay. We have been inseparable ever since. I smile and then feel the vacuum. The smile fades. This is the part of the expedition I don't like at all. When we parted back on Racquette Lake, she presented me with the two charms that I now hold to my chest. One is a silver heart saying, "You are Loved." The other, shaped to reflect its message, is inscribed "The Key to My Heart." I welled up with tears when she gave these to me. Now I am comforted as I drift off to dream of beautiful Nicole with flowing hair and striking blue eyes.

Like flipping pancakes, I rotate my frozen-stiff paddling clothes on the beach in the early morning sun. Watching my apparel steam its way to wearable is a comfort, while I brew up a cup of Adventurous Joe's Breakfast Blend and eat oatmeal. My appetite is back with a vengeance. I make another helping.

Coffee and breakfast eagerly devoured, paddling gear melted and warmed, I suit up and push the canoe from shore. A pair of mallard ducks paddle by with indifference, allowing me to pass close enough to see the male's striking green head, iridescent hues of blue on wing feathers and orange feet kicking away beneath the surface. The morning is calm and the sky a sublime deep blue, almost the cobalt blue seen at high altitudes, although this is far from it at only ninety-eight feet above sea level, the lowest point of the Northern Forest Canoe Trail.

Life as a nomadic expedition paddler starkly contrasts with the frenetic, multi-tasking life I managed to construct for myself back in the civilized, or real world, as they call it. Out here in the natural world, or what *I* think of as the real world, life is distilled into a few simple tasks that cannot be rushed or reprioritized. Travel, sustain myself and make a point of not dying, is all I *can* do. It's like *Groundhog Day*: wake up someplace beautiful, drink coffee, eat, review the day's float plan, dress for the conditions, pack, paddle, snack every hour, paddle, eat lunch, paddle, snack every hour, paddle, find a campsite, change out of wet clothes and hang on rescue rope drying line, make camp, make dinner, hang food (to give critters a challenging project), write in journal, sleep, wake and repeat. I love it.

Travel in moving water is interesting, and whitewater rapids provide a jolt of adrenaline with their speed and obstacles, requiring quick thinking and immediate actions that spice things up considerably. When the ocean is in a feisty mood, my pulse quickens, I become gravely serious and focused, and grip the paddle tighter.

Flatwater river, lake, or calm ocean paddling, on the other hand, provide a completely different experience. There is method to what, at times, feels like madness. I establish visual waypoints along my route and paddle from one to the next to the next. My stroke cadence determines the rhythm of breathing and heart rate. Call it trance-like or Zen-like, my mind seems to transcend my body; to leave it alone to do its work; viewing the scene from above. As if detached completely, my consciousness takes excursions, sometimes to ponder heady things, but usually to focus on the next stepping stone: a distant point of land, a boulder, a buoy or a lighthouse. I am unaware that I'm leaving a trail of wake and paddle swirls on the surface that immediately dissolve, leaving no trace of my passing. On the calmest days, paddling feels like I'm suspended in space. I become delirious and have, at times, almost fallen asleep. At one and the same time, it can be mind-numbing, peaceful and beautiful; even euphoric.

Later in the day, I begin my first upstream push, ascending the Missisquoi River. For now, I'm being treated to another mesmerizing paddle where the sky and water meld together on the horizon making each indistinguishable from the other. I smile, realizing that I am well enough to appreciate it.

CHAPTER FIVE

— Against the Flow —

The paddle north up Lake Champlain takes me along miles of randomly constructed seawalls. It's either poor siting of houses, or the lake's shoreline is on a rapid inland march. Nearly every structure is perched so near the water it's evident some have limited futures. A couple of them look like it would be wise for the residents to sleep wearing life jackets.

To delay the inevitable, every form of seawall has been constructed, from cement buttresses to giant boulders dumped into the lake. In some cases, there is a little of each. With houses jammed so close together, each having its own version of seawall, the shoreline is utterly chaotic to the eye. I pick up my stroke rate.

I pass under the Route 78 highway bridge and enter the upper portion of Champlain and the Missisquoi National Wildlife Refuge. This landscape starkly contrasts with the Lego-studded shoreline now behind me. The mouth of the river fans out into multiple wooded channels as it enters the lake, making the shortest route anything but obvious. I round a bend into the river, and can't believe my eyes. I have never seen a great blue heron rookery as big as this in my life, and I've seen some big ones. It's the Shad Island Heron Rookery, with scores of leafless trees hosting giant treetop nests of branch and twig. Stick-figured parents silhouetted against blue sky stand watch. Beaks point in my direction, and hundreds of eyes appraise my approach. Unconcerned with my passing beneath, not a bird moves so much as a feather. A spectacular, oddly silent scene.

The guidebook says that the Missisquoi River water is too polluted with agricultural runoff even to filter it for drinking. A water filter removes harmful organisms that can make people sick, but apparently it can't remove chemicals from fertilizers and pesticides. Of course, I anticipated this and filtered water into my MSR Dromedary bags before leaving camp on the lake in early morning. I have a safe supply, but what about the herons and other wildlife? If the water isn't safe enough for human consumption, even with filtering, then why is it okay for them to live in it, feed from it and raise their young in it? Wouldn't it be harmful to them? And doesn't this poison end up in the lake and beyond? A wave of disappointment comes over me. We can do better. Much better.

Thus far, there has been no real upstream paddling. All that is about to change. There are 162 miles of upstream travel on the Trail, two-thirds of it within Vermont and Quebec. The single longest stretch is the Missisquoi River from Lake Champlain in Vermont to Mansonville, Quebec, about seventy-four miles.

As I leave the rookery behind, I can feel the resistance. It requires more effort to keep the scenery passing at the same rate. There is a strong flow coming down the river. Perhaps I'll be able to paddle up some stretches of whitewater that would otherwise have to be tracked (walking and dragging the boat) at lower water. On the other hand, I'm ready for something different and I'm anxious to work my lower body.

Like most New England rivers, the Missisquoi has been exploited for hydroelectric power generation and has many dams to be portaged. Some are short, quick portages and some are longer and more strenuous. The portage at Sheldon Springs Dam is so steep that all other portages on the Trail are measured against it. It's a wonder that power company workers can drive down the hill in winter. I wouldn't be surprised if a couple of cars have gone for a swim.

Before I get there, I'll be spending the night in the snow on a campsite at the foot of Highgate Falls Dam. The site is reported to have a single tent pad and toilet on the hillside. I'm excited. Anytime I'm not leaning up against a log with a pile of pre-folded TP beside me, filling a disposable Wag Bag, I'm excited.

I'm reminded again that being pre-season on the Trail means that some facilities have not yet been repaired or maintained. I find the tent pad, clear it of branches fallen throughout winter, and set up my shelter. I take a look around but don't see the toilet. I go for a walk and cast about the area for likely locations. Nothing. I give up and venture down the hill closer to the river, following a branch-littered path. There it is, a toilet. Just a toilet sitting in a clearing overlooking the river. No walls, no door, no roof. I don't know what happened to the structure, but the only thing there is a wooden throne in the great wide open, facing the river. I use it, in the blowing snow. A bit drafty, but a memorable view.

At first light, I poke my head out of the tent. It is a winter wonderland. Confectioner's sugar has been delicately sprinkled over every tree limb and every inch of ground. The canoe, lying on its side, is now white with gently falling flakes. I look at my paddling gear, hung on the rescue rope drying line. There it all hangs. Not just my pfd and drysuit, but all the insulating layers; stiff as a board, covered with snow. Can't wait to put them on.

It must be the nutrients in the water from agricultural runoff that makes the rocks so damned slippery with algae. When I am unable to paddle up a rapid and have to track up on foot, I can't get a good foothold. I slip forward and back, and side to side. It's more than twice the work. There is scum all over the rocks, slippery as crap. I'm convinced that is actually the cause: cow crap.

I'm grateful to have sturdy river shoes, providing the ankle support I need to avoid injury. Using a trekking pole as a wading staff to prod the bottom, I steady myself. My other hand is holding the canoe by the bow deck plate. I can lean on it heavily. In combination, I'm pretty stable and move along quickly. When I do slip, I try not to curse, and instead remind myself that I'm having fun. I actually don't like it at all. Whenever I have a chance to paddle, rather than walk, I paddle. Even if it is slower.

The shadows are growing long and I have not yet seen signs of the next town, where my lodging awaits. I'm more than ready. Upstream travel on the Missisquoi is a mix of eddy-hopping up rapids by paddling up the slower current behind rocks, then bursting into the oncoming current and up into the next eddy, connecting them like stepping up a staircase. Where that isn't possible in featureless, swift sections, tracking-up is required and the lousy footing makes for a tough slog. It is exhausting. I'm ready to see Enosburg Falls and the Sterling Hotel so I can call an end to this interminable day.

The temperature feels like thirty-three degrees; just above freezing. I'm soaked with sweat from the upstream grunt and I'm chilled. I finally make it to the day's take-out and wheel the canoe the half-mile-or-so to the old hotel. I am grateful the Sterling has a restaurant and bar, although their best beers are in bottles.

The Sterling Hotel is a little rough but totally passes; a relic with musty old wood, creaky floor boards and bathroom fixtures dating back to Teddy Roosevelt, maybe beyond. The room is very basic with its most notable feature being a floor-to-ceiling mural painted across one entire wall, depicting a Vermont mountain scene with farms and downhill skiers. This place might not have an indoor water park, but the Sterling sure beats the Comfort Inn when it comes to local authenticity and warmth. I spread my wet gear throughout the bathroom and bedroom, crank up the heat, and scurry to the restaurant for a massive dinner and a beer. Not in that order.

Two older men, obvious frequent fliers at this establishment, are holding stools down at the bar. I'm the only other customer in the place and clearly a curiosity. On the television perched over the liquor bottles, Fox News commentators are body-slamming presidential candidate Hillary Clinton while heralding billionaire party-crasher Donald Trump. I feel that, *Yer not from around here, are ya, boy,* kind of vibe. The silence is awkward, so I dive into the water, hoping it's deep enough.

"I've been living out of my canoe since April 16th and have no idea what's going on with the election campaign," I say.

"You're not missing anything," says the nearest man. The other shakes his head. Ice broken, we start talking and I'm relieved by where the conversation goes.

As soon as I explain to them what I am doing, they ask me if I'd been sprayed by any manure spreaders while paddling up river. I can see that they're deadly serious. Next, they feed off each other and start ranting about how the State of Vermont is negligent in allowing agricultural practices that pollute the river. They point out that the Missisquoi River is basically pollution-free when it crosses into Vermont from

Quebec. After that, it suffers from chemical and nutrient pollution. I point out that even a water filter isn't sufficient to make it suitable for human consumption. They both nod, shake their heads and take another sip of their Bud Lites.

Straight out of a Norman Rockwell painting, the grizzled old men in blaze orange hunting caps, likely in their eighties, both sport flannel shirts. One has his pipe stem poking from a breast pocket. They talk about Canadian regulations that prohibit certain agricultural activities near the River, and do not allow cattle to be physically in the river or tributary streams in order to keep their effluent at a distance so the ground can filter it. They have a warmth about them and their perspectives are a breath of fresh air. Much better air than I breathed earlier as I paddled by manure spreaders flinging their goodness on the fields. I'm in a very rural town with two old codgers advocating for stricter environmental regulations to improve water quality. I'm warming up to Vermonters.

Three bottles of beer and a healthy portion of homemade chicken parmesan prepared by the owner disappear in a flash. I head to my room, swing the heavy, squeaky-hinged door closed behind me, slide the deadbolt in place, flop onto the bed and pass out. Still clothed.

Early sunlight filters through a parting in the curtains. I open one eye, then the other. I feel rested. I wake up wearing my birthday suit, but don't remember shedding clothes or climbing under the covers.

After removing clothing from around the room, most of it dry, I take a quick shower and make breakfast in the bathroom. The owner would no doubt have a fit if she saw me heating water with an open flame in this old tinderbox. She doesn't need to know.

Today will be another day of upstream travel, with one more to follow. The flow has been high enough that I've been able to paddle up many sections. At lower water, I am sure that through-paddlers need to either track up or carry. Good luck so far.

A cool breeze picks up as I pack the wheels into the canoe and launch. It's a headwind, but not too strong. Scattered clouds seem to pick up pace as they are swept toward the horizon, revealing a canopy of blue. It's below freezing. My fingertips are numb. Now it's time to enjoy the warming effect that paddling provides. A pair of Canada geese splash down on the river ahead as I leave the quaint Vermont town in my rearview. I'm sure it will be a good day.

With all this upstream travel, I find myself getting lazy. Too lazy to switch paddles. I paddle up swift, flatwater sections and even rapids with the lightweight, carbon, bent-shaft paddle instead of switching to the heavier, sturdier, Werner Bandit spoon-bladed whitewater stick. It's a practice that I know intellectually is not likely to be sustainable.

Approaching Richford, Vermont on this now blustery, cold, cloudless, afternoon, I aggressively work my way up a rapid. The current is strong and I have a good line with lots of momentum through to the top of the rapid. I'm breaking out into the slower water above the top drop when, in mid-stroke, I strike an unseen rock with the blade. It's a super-powerful stroke and the instant I hit the rock, the carbon paddle is severed at mid-blade. It goes completely flaccid, as if I have no blade at all on the end of the shaft. Reaching down to paddle with my bare hand would be more effective.

In one fluid motion, I jam the trashed paddle up front and grab the whitewater paddle from its clip mounts in front of me. I only miss one stroke and dig hard to keep momentum and explode upstream, narrowly avoiding a sideways broach on the rock above which I've been ferrying. I realize that if I had been at all slower with the paddle replacement, I'd have broadsided and right now would be perched on the rock with the canoe wrapped around it like a taco shell, ending the expedition with a horrifying crunch. I have to be smarter and do the right things, even if it takes more effort.

Another cold night spent in a warm motel would be a good thing. Hot restaurant food and cold beer sound good too. I check in at The Crossing Motel in Richford, Vermont and ask about securing the canoe overnight. The desk clerk suggests wheeling it straight into my room, so across the street I go. It fits with about two feet to spare. After a decent dinner at the bar, the best beer in a week, and a good night's sleep, I'll be ready to cross into Canada and end the day in Mansonville, Quebec.

Borders are usually crossed by road, in vehicles. It's a bit unusual to have someone crawl up over a river bank wearing a drysuit and lifejacket with whistle, knife, radios and strobe light attached. After a couple of hours paddling and tracking upstream, I pull out on the US Customs side of the border and go inside just to let them know what I'm doing. The wiry, friendly-faced officer finds it necessary to take my passport and spend fifteen minutes on the computer while I fight catching a chill. What could he possibly be doing, and why? I don't know if he's Googling me, finishing Solitaire, or whatever. It seems unnecessary and I'm eager to get going. My patience is growing thin. I realize that I skipped my snacks.

Now I am good to go, so I cross the bridge over the river. Up a steep grade and a hundred yards upstream, I step into Canadian Customs where I'm met by an ample, down-to-business, no-screwing-around woman outfitted with guns, clubs, cuffs and badges, in front of whom I feel dwarfish. After asking a few questions and reviewing my passport, she asks where my canoe is. I motion back down the road and tell her it's on the river bank next to the US Customs office.

Staring right through me, she barks in my face, "You must present yourself to me here with your vehicle and your belongings."

I look over my shoulder, down the long hill to the bridge and the invisible extra hundred yards over the bank to the canoe. For a fraction of a second I think about what that would involve.

"I will do whatever you need me to do," I say.

"Really? You'd do that?" she asks. I nod sincerely, praying she'll show me mercy.

"It's your lucky day," she says, for the first time revealing some humanity. A rather nice smile cracks the veneer. "Since you're willing to drag your canoe and gear up here and since your birthday is just two days off of mine, way off in years of course, I'm not going to make you do that. Have a good stay in Quebec."

She hands me my passport. I feel like grabbing her and hugging her, but know that could result in me wearing the handcuffs hanging off her belt.

Portaging up the steep hill into Mansonville, Quebec reveals over-the-shoulder views of Jay Peak, the northern Vermont ski area known for getting dumped on with snow. The slopes are covered. It's still cold. I've yet to ski there and pledge to fix that someday. With no place in mind to stay, I stop by the small market in the village square. The four people in the store surround me after I park the canoe by the door and walk in, clad in a dry suit and wearing my pack. Again, I'm a curiosity.

I usually stumble around trying to speak the native language when visiting other cultures, but I'm so obviously American that somebody inevitably saves me by speaking English. I think people like that I try at least, so after I've provided the right amount of entertainment, they jump in to spare me further embarrassment. This time, I don't have a chance to make an attempt before the woman behind the register points to one of the twenty-something guys next to me and says, "He know English."

With his cap screwed onto his head sideways, he has the vibe of a European skateboarder and is dying to know where I came from and what I'm doing. He translates for his friends, who seem to be more amused than impressed. He informs me that there's no campground or lodging within canoe-dragging distance, and tells me that a nice older woman bought the white church across town with a guest room to rent.

"She's probably there. You should go knock on the door."

Dragging the canoe across the village green to the white church, I go to the arched, wooden side door, knock, and step back. The door doesn't budge, but a window slides open and a woman pokes her head out. I almost laugh. I'm in a scene from *The Wizard of Oz*. Next, she'll proclaim, "Orders are, nobody can see the Great Oz! Not nobody, not nohow!" Or maybe she's going to ask me what kind of ice cream cone I want.

I feel bad about my indiscretion and hope my face doesn't give away my thoughts. Her kind eyes draw me in, and she seems happy to have me here.

"Just a moment," she says, and opens the door.

Marie-Paule Villeneuve is a single woman in her fifties with a daughter in the States. She tells me that she recently bought the church and that I am one of her first guests. I ask her what possessed her to buy a church. She says she doesn't know, but it seemed like a good idea. She hopes. She takes me to the church rectory, which she has refitted as a guest room. There is a table outside, on which several novels are displayed, all written by the woman herself. Inside, it is very basic. It feels too small for the two of us, without violating the rules of personal space. For a tired paddler living out of a tent, it will definitely work.

We negotiate a price, which, to my surprise, is super reasonable. I ask about food but am told there's nothing within walking distance. She offers to take me to the nearest restaurant, two miles down the road. I eagerly take her up on it. Once there, she introduces me to a half dozen of her friends sitting at the bar. They test my French, then switch to English. Before leaving, she gives me her cell phone number so she can pick me up when I am finished. What an Angel.

I don't know why, but I wake with Keith Urban singing *John Cougar, John Deere, John 3:16* ringing through my head. I pull it up on YouTube and play it over and over while I make coffee and oatmeal in the room. It becomes the soundtrack to the Quebec portion of the trip. Can't get it out of my head, but that's not a bad thing.

After yesterday's upstream paddling and portaging, followed by a big dinner and three beers, apparently there's a lot I didn't notice before going to bed. It isn't until now that I realize that over the head of the rectory's double bed is a rectangular five-foot, one-way mirror overlooking rows of pews and the church's altar. I roll my eyes around the room, as thoughts of abhorrent church scandals flash through my head. There's that icky feeling. Goosebumps and prickly skin. I had never before spent the night in a church. Now that I've checked that box, I'm not sure if I will again.

I speed-brush my teeth, skip flossing, and quickly load my pack. I pull the canoe from behind the church and hit the road for the next put-in only a few hundred yards away. I'm happy to be outside, on my way. It's a cloudless, sunny, chilly day in Quebec. Well rested, off I go singing the song's chorus about never growing up, never growing old. It resonates.

CHAPTER SIX

— Over the Divide and Beyond —

A river's yawning mouth, disgorging its heavy volume into the next body of water, is a stark contrast with its narrow, meandering source that can make the act of floating a boat a challenge. I usually travel from a river's source, not toward it; in concert with its downstream rhythms; drifting with the current toward its end; watching it grow. Upstream travel has a unique way of showing every inch of the waterway as it shrinks to its point of origin. My toil is worthwhile and awakens me to the tiniest of details along the way: the textures of rocks, gravel and sand, the water plants beneath the surface, and those along shore.

As I carry the canoe up to the road for the almost six-mile Grand Portage into the next watershed, I look over my shoulder at the headwaters of the Missisquoi River. I smile to myself. Under wispy clouds painted across the morning sky, she elegantly twists between fields and woods, her sparkling waters softly disappearing around a distant bend from whence I came. I have an intimate relationship with her. I know every inch of her and exactly where she is going.

The height of land between the Missisquoi River and Lake Memphremagog watersheds affords views of Jay Peak, Vermont and the nearby Mont Owl's Head ski area here in Quebec. Trails on both are still covered in snow. I find an old woods road where I pull the canoe far enough off the paved road not to be seen. Slathering almond butter and strawberry jam onto a tortilla, I'm anticipating a quiet lunch in the woods, resting my legs. Before I get the tortilla rolled, a white 4X4 Chevy

Silverado pickup truck bounces its way up the ruts and parks eight feet away. An elderly man inches open the driver's door and rappels to the ground. He begins in French, then cocks his head to appraise me, and immediately switches to English.

"What are you doing?" he says.

"Making a sandwich."

"No, I mean with the canoe and all this gear."

I realize how confusing this scene must be. I'm sitting in the woods on top of a mountain, three miles from the nearest water and I have a seventeen-and-a-half-foot canoe loaded with gear.

I tell him my story and he offers me a ride to the lake. I gratefully decline the offer, and in turn, ask him what he's doing here.

"I was cutting some trees and my chainsaw broke. I had to go get a part so I can finish. Are you sure you won't accept a ride?" he says, dropping the tailgate to grab his saw.

"No, thank you. I'm doing this thing human powered, just like back in the day," I say.

Saw in hand, he brushes past me. He waves with the back of his hand as he walks away and says, "I think you're a little crazy. But have fun."

Quebec farmland is like Vermont farmland with different architecture. A rural European vernacular, the most conspicuous features are steeply sloping rooflines leading to upturned drip edges and gaudy-colored metal roofs. A Candy Land-like vibe. Finally at the lake, I'm floating once again. From Perkins Landing, I head south toward Vermont.

The international border is marked by a denuded swath of woods that bisects the lake. I pull over to the Canadian customs station, an unmanned white shack with a phone. I pick up the hand piece and it rings twice before being answered. The officer at some distant station grills me and seems to try to trip me up. I wonder if he's looking for an excuse to make a field trip. It's weird to pass through customs this way. I give him my passport number and wait in silence. This doesn't feel exactly like state-of-the-art border security.

"You're free to go," he says.

Who's going to stop me? I think.

The Trail guidebook says that, when I arrive at the marina in

Newport, Vermont, I need to check in with US Customs using the video phone at a kiosk. I walk up, towing the canoe, and discover that the place is undergoing renovations and I can't find a US Customs presence anywhere. On the boat ramp, a teenage boy in a Cabela's sweatshirt is drowning worms. He knows nothing of a video phone. I ask a young woman walking by, but she doesn't know either. I give up, and Google the Newport, Vermont police station. Following directions, I drag the canoe three blocks through town to the station. A police car follows me slowly for the last seventy-five yards and parks next to me. The officer gets out and asks me what I'm doing. I explain that I need to check-in with US Customs but can't find the video phone and that's a step I don't think I should skip. I ask if he can help.

"Just a minute," he says, sliding back into the cruiser to use his phone.

Five minutes later, I'm in the police station chatting with US Customs over the phone. I tell them my story, give them my passport information and I'm on my way. I reunite with the canoe in front of the station, and ask a twenty-something hipster shuffling by where the best beer taps are in town.

"The Ciderhouse on Main Street, right down there," he says pointing in my direction of travel.

I'm supposed to meet Nicole at a motel on the other side of town. She's driving from Maine and it's the first time I will have seen her since we parted that morning on the sand beach so many long days ago. Although I'm parched and can think of nothing more satisfying than a tall draught, I decide to pass on a stop at the Ciderhouse and walk on by, dragging the canoe.

Trying to shake the thought of a cold beer and refocus on seeing Nicole, I hear a female voice from behind.

"Hey, are you John Connelly?"

Little did I know, but this question would become a theme throughout my trip.

I stop dead in my tracks, and turn around to see a woman walking my way. She has a broad smile and when she arrives, reaches out with a hearty handshake.

"I'm Maria's mom. Maria from the Maine Island Trail Association.

She said you'd be coming through here. Want to join us for a beer?"

Some things are meant to be.

I park the canoe outside the Ciderhouse's picture window to keep an eye on it. I enjoy a locally brewed IPA while chatting with Maria's parents and their friends.

"What an unexpected pleasure," I say. "This has been wonderful, but I have to get going. I'm meeting Nicole for the first time in many days and I'd like to wash off a layer or two of sweat and grime before she arrives."

They pick up the check and shoo me out the door. Great people.

Canoe in tow, I make it to the motel, check-in and get cleaned up before Nicole arrives. I can barely contain my enthusiasm. Throughout the expedition, Nicole will intercept me nine times to provide me with supplies and spend time with me. I don't know how many hours or hundreds of miles she'll drive, but they are many. When I see the Jeep pull into the parking space next to the canoe, I run out, pull her out of the car, and hug her like I'll never let her go.

We take the following day to find the best food and drink around, lounge in the hot tub and catch up with each other.

When I get back on the water, the weather turns dank again. There is rain and days of cold air in the forecast. I spend the next two days ascending the Clyde River. It's not as slippery walking as the Missisquoi, but it's narrow, steeper and the water is high. Paddling up is only possible in short stretches, so the majority requires in-stream tracking. High water and branches stretching over the shallows force me to track up in knee-to-waist-deep rapids.

I track upstream around a bend, pass beneath a road bridge and notice broken fishing lines, bobbers and lures hanging from the bridge and strewn throughout nearby tree branches. My eye catches a strange silhouette rotating slowly in the breeze a couple yards ahead at eye level. In strong current, I skirt a large boulder using the canoe for support. I move closer. Having succumbed to the deadly web of fishing line, claws clenched, wings hanging at its side, the crow's glazed, empty stare is like an extinguished light as it spins round and round in the wind. I think of Alfred Hitchcock.

My slog upstream is complicated by leg-hold traps of car tires and wheels, camouflaged beneath the tannin colored water. It is sad that, over the years, this river has been used for dumping. There's automobile metal strewn about in places as well. I need to be careful or risk a detour to a hospital for a tetanus shot. The guidebook says the next portage trail has the distinction of going over an old, half-buried rusted car. As I near the trail in knee-deep water, I notice a ghostly figure swaying back and forth in the current. I step forward and bend down. It's the flayed, rotting carcass of a deer pinned between boulders in the current. So far, this has not been my favorite part of the trip.

I wheel the canoe up the road and portage the next dam, putting in on Pensioner Pond. The sun has set and it's hovering above freezing with a light rain. I paddle most of the pond and still can't find a legitimate campsite. At the far end, I see a house under construction. No lights on. I haul out and set up my tent next to their waterside boat house. It's inconspicuous enough, and I'll leave at first light. There's a portable toilet for the construction workers. It's unlocked. Bonus. This is my first "stealth" camping of the trip.

The upstream course alternates between long stretches of river and a series of ponds. Portages are mostly used to bypass hydro dams and the upper river is a web of meandering channels through flat swampland riddled with a dozen or so beaver dams that have to be hauled over. "Meander" doesn't say it. On my map, the river looks like someone with severe hand tremors squiggled the line. I feel like I'm paddling two miles to gain a half mile distance on the map. The route I just paddled is on my right and the part I'm paddling toward is on my left, flowing in the opposite direction. The current has carved channels in places, leaving islands. With all this zig-zagging I could paddle in circles forever, if not paying attention.

There's a small rapid with a single short drop up ahead. I pick up tempo and charge the eddy line at a fifteen-degree angle, easily attaining the drop into the slow, dense current above. Rounding a lefthand bend, I see a conspicuous red buoy ahead. As I get nearer, I see that it's no buoy. It's the end of a red Royalex canoe vertically pinned in the current. I paddle by, peering into the depths to see whether it's a torn off end or if it's still intact. For as deep as the murkiness will allow my view, it appears to be whole. It doesn't seem like sixteen feet of depth is possible in this spot, so more than likely there's another half at rest someplace on the bottom of the river. I glide by, release my paddle with one hand, pet my canoe and softly say, "Don't worry, I won't let that happen to you."

I realize I've missed it. It's clear from emerging rooftops of houses that the village of Island Pond where I plan to rest my head tonight is behind me. The river's headwaters are too narrow to turn the canoe around, so I back paddle through overhanging alders and twenty-five yards of hairpin bends made for a ten-foot canoe, to find where I went wrong. Beavers have dammed the outflow of the pond. The four-feet high edifice disburses water throughout a hundred-yard barricade of wiry alder trees with no other clear channels. I sidle up to the dam, lift the boat over to the other side, and in minutes am paddling under an old historic hotel built over the river, and out onto Island Pond where the last flicker of the day's light has faded to gray.

A few strokes later, I'm at Lakeside Motel where management has left me an envelope with my key. A hot shower, beer from the convenience store across the parking lot, and a carryout order of Italian food are in my future. In that order, too.

Up early. The morning is overcast with little wind, and a daytime high of fifty is forecast. It's expected to stay like this for the next day or so. I'm well fed and well rested. I've been looking forward to this day for months. When planning the trip, I learned that the Nulhegan River, to which I will portage over the watershed divide, and run later today, is a formidable whitewater river with two impassable gorges. It is a natural flow river with a relatively small watershed making flows often too low to navigate, so it's a section most folks carry around. But I'm thinking this is where the fun is. It's been raining for the past few days, so enough water shouldn't be an issue. It never occurs to me that there may be too much.

Portaging from the Clyde watershed to the Nulhegan has me anxious to get going. I put in by a roadside culvert near the source of the river, and follow its meandering route through the Silvio O. Conte National Fish and Wildlife Refuge with its abundant life. Geese sitting on their eggs drop their heads slightly and watch me pass. Seeing the marshland narrow and drop into boulder-strewn rapids quickens my pulse. From here, the river descends through two gorges requiring portaging, and many rapids later the Nulhegan ends its journey when it meets the Connecticut River almost twenty miles downstream. I'll be paddling a river from its source to its end in one day. One of my favorite things. It's not every day you get to do this.

The current picks up. I carve the inside of a dogleg turn to the left, and there it is. The white pine tree must be seventy feet. It's not tall anymore. It's stretched horizontally, completely blocking the River. Its branches reach deep into the current, sweeping up anything trying to float by. I back paddle so hard that the canoe reverses direction in a single stroke. Just two boat lengths upstream of the obstruction, I ferry toward the left shore; the only shore where a portage would be possible. I scan the menacing branches for a clear path through, or at least one that's clear enough. I see it briefly and, just as quickly, it's gone. Then I see it again. The opening appears and disappears with the undulating current.

I continue to back paddle, hold my position, and assess what a portage would look like. It looks ugly: steep bank, mud and more downed trees on shore. The river pulses and the sketchy path through reveals itself again. Decision made. I time my approach. Now. I push the bow through the opening and pull hard on one last stroke for momentum. Quickly throwing the paddle into the boat, I reach forward, grab branches on either side and pull hard, while turning my head to avoid making shish kabobs of my eyeballs on the skewers of branches raking my face. Broken ends fill the boat. Wet limbs bending against the canoe's fiberglass gunwales screech like nails on a chalkboard. I manage to make it all the way in a single motion. Behind me, the river slams the opening shut. I'm through.

Immediately in front, glacial erratic boulders in the river mark the beginning of the whitewater rapids that will continue to the river's end in the Connecticut. The shoreline rocks are underwater. The river is swollen and pitching downhill, creating three-foot high waves and a minefield of scattered pour-over holes that must be avoided. This is more dramatic than I imagined.

By nailing clean lines, the boat remains dry as I whip into the large eddy, marking the mandatory portage above the first gorge. This canoe performs well in rapids as long as I don't ask it to make sudden changes of direction. If I approach the whitewater as if in a decked downriver or wildwater racing canoe, choose the fastest, cleanest lines well in advance, work with the currents that require only the subtlest of turns, this should go well. A miscalculation or lapse of concentration could be disastrous. I can't let either happen.

After the carry of the first gorge, I munch on some Grandy Oats trail mix and look downstream at the next stretch of rapids. The terrain makes it impractical to walk downstream to scout the drop. The guidebook says to portage the falls and continue. That suggests that everyone must routinely run what lies below. Right? How bad could it be?

I look more closely. The river turns ninety degrees to the right. There's a clear horizon line, above which spray is rising several feet into the air. A minuscule break in the overcast sends a narrow ray of light into the mist. An iridescent rainbow appears for an instant and disappears as the clouds mend the hole. I laugh at the thought of Skittles and strap my helmet back on, snug up my pfd, slide into the boat, and pull on thigh straps. This is going to be interesting.

At the outflow of the gorge, the river is only a few yards wide, moving ten miles per hour or better. Facing upstream in the left shore eddy, I take a half stroke forward, offering my bow to the oncoming wall of water. The river grabs the end of the canoe and sends it downstream. A bow draw stroke pulls us into the main flow, followed with a forward stroke, which sends us full speed downriver with the current. Bearing down on the hard-right turn ahead, I need to mend my angle to the right, cutting the turn as close as possible to the inside. With the current forcing itself to the outside of the turn, it'll be impossible to push against if I need to be further right. It's best to go tightly to the inside and then, if necessary, adjust to the outside with the current instead of trying to go against its inertia.

The drop roars louder with each stroke. I feel exhaled wind from the huge river-wide hydraulic as I near the lip. I feel wet spray on my face. It smells earthy. As I round the inside of the corner, I see that

I'm in the perfect spot. The bow drops down a smooth tongue of dark water, either side of which is nothing but roiling whitewater that would swamp the canoe in an instant. Immediately to my right, the river falls between boulders that would ruin the canoe and my day. With a single stroke, I pull clear of the ledge drop. In front of me are continuous rapids with large waves and a minefield of holes to avoid. Not a single rock is exposed. I've scored high water on the Nulhegan.

It's coming at me too fast. Furiously, I read the rapids ahead to pick straightforward lines avoiding last second turns. I feel like a hockey goalie at slap shot practice. I've got to make it stop a minute; take a breath. Teardrop-shaped shoreline eddies dot the nearby rocky right bank. I quickly back paddle, ferry into a micro-eddy and hang onto a conveniently placed boulder, still facing downstream. The crux of this portion of the river appears to be behind me, so I relax slightly to soak it all in.

There is beauty in the river's chaos and flow, the spirit of its determination to flee the mountains and head to the sea. Moist air fills my nostrils. The boulder I'm grasping is cool and damp to the touch, and the canoe rocks against it with the pulsing of the rapid. In the moment, I'm mesmerized and frozen in time.

The sudden realization of my situation is like a slap across the face. I snap out of it. I'm all by myself in a very remote place, running high water rapids I've never seen and can't scout, in a boat that is minimally maneuverable at best. I can't afford to make even the smallest mistake. I tap this energy for strength, not apprehension, and try to think about it differently. I've got it. I'm with other paddlers. I'm in the lead, showing them the routes through rapids. I'm not really alone, I'm the leader. This fantasy is a framework for boosting confidence. I just have to remember not to look behind me.

I tackle more whitewater, complete a portage of the second gorge, and then there are miles of continuous rapids to the confluence where the Nulhegan merges with the Connecticut.

Within sight of the big river, I pitch tent, inflate the pad and fluff my sleeping bag for later. After draping wet paddling gear over the rescue rope strung between birch trees, I boil water to reconstitute a dehydrated dinner. The weather is overcast and cool, but I'm warmed to the core from the energy and richness of the day. Best vacation ever.

Downstream travel on the Connecticut River flies by on an impressive flow volume. Ahead of schedule, I arrive at the mouth of New Hampshire's Upper Ammonoosuc River. Its flow is a fraction of the big river's but the Upper Ammo's banks are full. The canoe comes to a full stop in the current despite brisk paddling. There are no eddies or water features to aid upstream paddling. The current is uniform from bank to bank. This is going to be tough. The joy of downstream paddling is over. It will be many days before I see a single drop of water heading in the right direction.

The New Hampshire section of the Trail is upstream travel on two rivers: the Upper Ammo and Androscoggin. The Upper Ammo's nineteen miles from Groveton to Gord's Corner Store in West Milan takes effort. There are short portages around dams, but paddling and tracking up rapids with this much water proves relentless and takes more time, denying me the approved campsite I targeted for tonight.

Night falls and I am still two miles from my planned overnight destination. I go into stealth mode. I need to make myself invisible to landowners and passersby on the road paralleling the river. I drag the canoe through seventy-five yards of long, browned grass clumps, mashed from winter snow, then erect my shelter among scraggly bushes. Next to this home for the night is a lightly worn game trail, bordered by small alder trees with frayed bark and grooved rake marks from a testosterone-saturated, whitetail buck several long months ago.

A damp chill settles in as I clean my dish and utensil by headlamp. Snuggled into my sleeping bag, I lie looking at the ceiling and think about the prospect of sleep, but the clumps of grass under the tent feel like large balls of yarn placed indiscriminately under my sleeping pad. I push and prod the balls to sculpt a form for my tired bones, but soon realize that I'm better off filling the spaces with articles of clothing. It's far from ideal, but I pass out quickly.

I awake to another overcast morning. The first light is dim, and I feel as if I'm not alone. I pry open my eyes. I'm right. The miniature pumpkin seed with eight tiny oars rows itself across the no-see-um netting six inches from my face. It takes a second to focus. I'm hopeful that the spring's first tick is on the outside of the net. I bolt into action, stripping off the sleeping bag. No clothes to worry about. I initiate a thorough tick check, wishing I had eyes in the back of my head. The last thing I need is a debilitating disease. Sometimes you don't realize you've been bitten, so for the next three days I'll check every nook and cranny of my topography for the telltale sign of Lyme disease: that horrid little red bullseye of a rash.

After another day of foiling the Upper Ammo's efforts to slow progress, I ascend the river's North Branch and finally arrive at Gord's Corner Store. This marks the end of facing off with the Upper Ammo, and the beginning of a four-mile-or-so march over the watershed divide to join the Androscoggin River. Just like the river I leave behind, this will play obstructionist to my efforts in reaching its headwaters.

With the canoe parked outside the store, I pull open the doors and am delighted to see that they sell beer and serve food cooked on their grill. A man approaches me.

"Are you John Connelly?" he says.

I confirm, and learn that I have just met the store's namesake who helps maintain the section of Upper Ammo I have just ascended. He welcomes me and explains that a Trail representative told him I was the first through-paddler, so he was expecting to see me at some point.

I ask about nearby camping and gladly accept Gord's offer to camp beneath an apple tree behind the store. He points out the portable toilet at the edge of the parking lot. This is deluxe compared to last night's situation in the tick field. I order two cheeseburgers with everything, along with a chicken sandwich, and his wife slaps the patties on the grill. I spot a good IPA and grab a six pack. While the grill sizzles, I decide on the four breakfast sandwiches I will order in the morning before I hit the road.

I rise at first light and crank up the stove. With freshly brewed coffee in hand, I round the side of the store to head for the portable toilet. Why the hell do they have to call it a Porta-John? A father and his son, both dressed in camouflage gear, are watching the boy's wild turkey being measured and weighed at the store's game check-in station. The boy, who looks all of twelve years old, beams with pride as the bird is placed next to him on the tailgate. He fans the tail feathers for a photo op, dwarfed by the bird. I ask him if it's his first turkey. He nods with equal measures of excitement and humility. I congratulate him. I remember how I felt when I got my first turkey. I was forty-seven.

Finally, a day with sun and warmth. What a spectacular day for carrying to the Androscoggin River and pulling my way upstream. It's a twenty-three-mile day if I'm to make my destination of Errol, New Hampshire at the river's headwaters. Three times, pickup trucks stop to see if I want a ride to the river. Three times, I gratefully decline. Three times, I'm told that I'm nuts.

During the time I've been on this expedition, waterfowl parents have gone from incubating their eggs on nests, to ushering newly-hatched ducklings and goslings around their new world. Now the babies, covered in yellow, downy fuzz, have their first pin feathers poking through.

It's good to be afloat again. I paddle up the Pontook Reservoir, a section of the Androscoggin plugged by a large dam. I hear an awful commotion off to my right, so paddle into a large cove, where I witness something remarkable.

The shrieking and honking is deafening. A violent battle for survival is taking place. Like a war plane on a bombing run, a bald eagle tucks and dives from the cover of a blinding sun to make an assault. As it pulls up, the raptor extends its talons toward the target. Broad wings flapping wildly, a mother goose screams at the top of her lungs, running across the water in the direct path of the attacker. Four goslings scatter into the cattails at water's edge. One hundred percent committed, the two converging birds almost collide. The eagle's attack thwarted, mother goose retreats to gather her young, and the eagle settles atop a nearby white pine. There's nothing but time. It'll wait for another opportunity. An eerie calm settles over the cove. I return to my upstream trek. Clearly, this drama is not over.

The river is high, but I prefer to paddle up rapids rather than walk the road, although it takes longer and requires much more effort. I make my destination well before dark. The manager of the Northern Waters campground and whitewater school on the Upper Androscoggin in

Errol offers me a riverside campsite. Gratefully, I accept. Now, I have calories to replace. I set up my tent, hang my wet clothes and walk into town to find taps and to gorge myself. I'll sleep like a log.

If I become shipwrecked on a deserted island or sent adrift in a life raft, lost at sea for seventy-six days like fellow Mainer, Stephen Callahan, when his sailboat sank crossing the Atlantic, I would have good reason to emerge at the end of this trek with a beard to my chest and dreadlocks to my shoulders. With what lies ahead, I still have plenty of opportunity for that, but I'll do my best to avoid it. So far, I've managed to maintain my appearance, thanks to my battery-powered beard clippers and razor. Instead of using my reflection in still water to get the hedge trimmed properly, I use the emergency signal mirror that's stuffed in my pfd pocket. I intend to present as well as possible when Nicole intercepts me with re-provisions. No Jeremiah Johnson or Grizzly Adams. I don't think she's prepared to see that. I'll whack away at my face in the morning.

One of the things I love about wilderness travel is that you can never know for sure what the day will bring. The portage above the upper river into Lake Umbagog follows a paved road. With backpack straps snugged, I pull the canoe on its cart up the hill.

As I approach a bend in the road, I hear the rapid clip-clop of hooves. They're getting louder. Fast. A giant bull moose rounds the bend and breaks into a full-on gallop. Hooves pound the pavement, then are muffled on the dirt shoulder, then back to the hardtop. His head darts from side to side, crazed eyes searching for an escape route. He's closing fast.

From years of adventuring in Maine's North Woods, I've had many moose experiences and am well familiar with the beasts. One winter evening I totaled one with my Isuzu Trooper. The car made out only marginally better than the moose, but at least a needy family was able to fill its freezer. Another time, one jumped in front of my mountain bike, blinding me with a layer of mud, sending me over the handlebars. I've had a one-antlered bull run within two feet of me down a snowmobile trail while I stood motionless on my cross-country skis hoping he wouldn't turn the antlered side toward me on the way by. On another occasion, one tripped over the guy lines of my tent while I was in it. I surprised a cow moose who chased me down a dirt road, shooing me away from her two calves. I've paddled next to them on rivers. For twenty minutes, I stood within five feet of a noble bull on top of a mountain, while I chatted to him and we both watched the sun set.

By now, I can pretty much tell what's running through their minds. There are only two things that would make this bull run my way at full throttle: an even bigger bull, which isn't likely because this guy is pretty damned big, or a vehicle.

Only twenty yards of moist morning air separates me from a thousand pounds of speeding woods beef. I'm clearly not on his radar screen. Dropping the end of the canoe, I yell at the top of my lungs, waving both arms frantically to break his trance. We lock eyes. He hesitates, throws his head to the right and crashes his way into the woods. Disaster averted. Two seconds later, a Ford F-150 pickup rounds the bend.

CHAPTER SEVEN

— Back Home for the First Time —

Lake Umbagog straddles the border of New Hampshire and Maine. I have been waiting for weeks to return to Maine. There's something about simply going over the border that makes me feel like I've come home.

The day is spent crossing the lake into my home state, then carrying a rough 3.2 miles up the Rapid River. Unfortunately, today is upstream travel. This is one of my favorite rivers. Nicole and I try to paddle it once a year. It is continuous and steep, with about two miles of rapids. It is remote, so never overly busy with paddlers, even on dam release days with good water. Our friends have a cabin on Lower Richardson Lake above the river at Middle Dam. I'll meet them and Nicole there for an evening of camaraderie and large quantities of good food.

As I end the carry and approach the dam, I hear yelling. I see three figures running my way, waving their arms. Much to my delight, it turns out that they are carrying a backpack of my favorite beer.

It's great to be back in Maine traveling in familiar watersheds. It feels comfortable. After coffee and a mountain of pancakes with Maine maple syrup, I launch onto Lower Richardson into a stiff breeze, waves wanting to be whitecaps, and drizzle. I'm already looking forward to when next I'll see Nicole. It is not easy leaving her standing on the shore waving goodbye. I'll never get used to it. Little do I know, but this will be my most challenging day yet. And potentially deadly.

The drizzle ends and the wind dies. Halfway to the next portage at Upper Dam on Upper Richardson Lake, I approach a familiar landmark. The camp sits on a hillside back from the water. I've stayed there once before for a whitewater weekend on the Rapid. My friend and I hadn't planned to meet on my way through, but I'm hopeful he's there.

I'm in luck. Ben Pearson, day pack slung over his shoulder, is walking toward the boat house. I call out. He stops and squints hard.

"Is that John Connelly?" he shouts and scurries to the dock where I pull up.

Ben is a fellow member of the L.L.Bean *Alumni Association.* Now in retirement, he spends time at camp when not off adventuring in Alaska, Quebec, or some other wild place. We chat for a few minutes and then I'm on my way.

The rain returns in earnest as I portage Upper Dam and put-in on Mooselookmeguntic Lake. I round the point, and face a yawning six miles of open water separating me from my destination and the next portage. The morning's forecast indicated a cold front moving through later in the day, but nothing extreme. Current conditions look benign enough to abandon any thought of hugging the shoreline for wind protection. That would add miles to the day and in these conditions, it's not necessary. I take a direct line across the expanse and paddle with purpose. Two miles into it, all hell breaks loose. The front is vicious and kicks up steep three-foot breaking waves, threatening to sink the canoe and turn my fate into a news headline.

By tapping into my whitewater skills, I complete the crossing. I'm exhausted, but oddly energized by the realization that I've made it with only three gallons of water in the boat. Less than a half mile to go, I take a short rest on the leeward side of the mainland. When the front blew in, rain changed to sleet, and now it's snowing so hard I can barely make out the boat landing in Oquossoc, the end of the day's paddling. I hope Nicole can save my bacon.

From repeatedly freezing my hands, I'm cursed with capillaries that refuse to carry blood to my fingers. I work the paddle loose from clenched fingers, and have to make a deliberate effort to peel off the neoprene gloves. There's no sensation in my fingers, so operating the phone is a challenge. I'm not hypothermic, but I'm conscious of the fact that I'd better start paddling soon to stay ahead of the curve. Having returned from our rendezvous on Lower Richardson, Nicole has been home in Falmouth for a couple of hours and is delighted to get my call. I brief her on my ordeal and she's appalled. I'm sure she can hear the wind in the speaker and the chilled edge in my voice. She promises to find me a warm, dry place to sleep.

I wheel the canoe down the mile-long road to Rangeley Lake, and a big shiny four-wheel- drive pickup heading in my direction pulls off the side of the snowy road. From out of the cab, a tall, good looking man wearing a puffy, down jacket has a spring in his step.

"Are you John Connelly?" he asks.

I can't help but smile. Nicole has worked her magic again. Kevin introduces himself and tells me about Nicole calling to get me a room.

"We're not open this early in the season, but you have one of our suites. We're taking Mom out for a Mother's Day dinner, but the suite is ready for you and the door's unlocked."

He passes me a square of paper with directions.

"There's a bowl of homemade chicken noodle soup in the fridge. We should be home early enough that I can lend you the pickup so you can head into town to get a late dinner. I'd ask you if you want a ride, but Nicole says you're going to refuse. Is that right?"

I nod my head and reference my human powered thing.

"You might be just a little crazy, but I like that," he says.

The Trail Angel named Kevin heads off, and the rattling of diesel engine fades in air thick with dancing wet snowflakes. I fold the directions to Rangeley Lake Cruises and Kayaking into the pocket of my life-jacket and continue down the road. Now I have a spring in *my* step.

I sleep like a rock. This morning, I treat myself to a double portion of Grandy Oats oatmeal sprinkled with nuts, and swill a full twelve-cup pot of Adventurous Joe Coffee instead of the typical two cups. It's going to be another cold one; another gray day with temps in the high twenties. Winds are predicted at twenty, gusting to thirty out of the west. I will have a tailwind to the town of Rangeley. A glance out the window confirms the forecast. Tiny snowflakes streak sideways but never land,

and there are two-foot waves in the cove. Time to suit up.

Under ten miles, today will be one of my shortest days of paddling. Once to Rangeley, it's about a three-mile carry over the watershed divide to the South Branch of the Dead River. I'll have to camp in blowing snow if I go that far today. A warm, dry night under a roof at the Rangeley Inn is a much better plan. I chip an inch of ice out of the bottom of the canoe before putting in on Rangeley Lake. Let's get this done. There's a decent tap selection waiting.

The biggest reason for starting the expedition so early in spring is to catch the highest water possible on natural flow rivers, especially the Dead's south branch. If this river is not high enough, a three-mile carry to the put-in is followed by an additional twenty miles of hiking with the canoe. I know that I need plenty of good karma, and I'm anxious to know how this turns out.

Unrelenting days of rain, and now melting snow, turn out to be my salvation. I arrive at the put-in on the South Branch of the Dead River. There is *just* enough water and not one drop more. At minimum boatable flow, I'm spared the twenty-mile walk to Flagstaff Lake in Stratton.

I haul up and over downed trees in the early flatwater section. The riverbed now tilts and the current picks up for the rest of the trip to the lake. Just above Fansanger Falls Gorge, worthy of scouting, I pull out on river right. The water is too low to run the initial drop without subjecting the canoe to an awful beating. I need a better look at what's below, so climb the bank to the road.

One of the few cars to travel this remote piece of asphalt today comes to an abrupt halt, backs up and parks on the shoulder. Flashers on, the driver opens his door and shuffles over.

"Are you John Connelly?" he says.

"Yes," I say, thinking that this is getting absurd.

"My name is John, too, and I'm the Northern Forest Canoe Trail maintainer for this section of the Trail. I heard that you were heading this way. Want to spend the night at our house on Flagstaff Lake? It's on your way and we'll make dinner."

I can't believe my good fortune. John explains how to find their house. I take mental note.

"We're hiking up Saddleback Mountain today," he says. "We'd have missed you if we had remembered our trekking poles and hadn't had to go back home to get them. I guess everything happens for a reason,"

Slamming the car door, he waves and drives off.

The remainder of the river is mostly rapids winding through forests of hardwoods and softwoods, passing over ledges, between boulders and over gravel bars. Bald eagles are everywhere. Fish scatter in all directions as I ply the waters of the last two rapids. It's hard to tell exactly what they are, but I assume suckers. I round the last corner, where the river opens up spectacularly into Flagstaff Lake with tall mountains as backdrop. I am taken aback by the sheer number of bald eagles perched in trees, soaring circles over the rapids, and sitting on stream-side rocks. The buffet is open. Glad I'm not a fish.

John and his wife treat me to a wonderful meal and conversation. Recently, John gave up drinking, but still has a fridge full of India Pale Ales. With an invitation to help myself, looks like I lucked out again.

After a sound night's sleep, I am up bright and early. John helps me put the canoe in from his dock and I'm off. It's sunny and much warmer than it has been in weeks. I paddle onto Flagstaff Lake, continuing along the foot of the Bigelow Mountain Range rising above the south shore.

Flagstaff Lake has a sad history. When the dam was built to provide storage for hydroelectric dams downstream, two villages were handed a death sentence, and now sit beneath the reservoir. Residents were forced to evacuate and bodies were exhumed from cemeteries. At high lake levels, there is no evidence of this past. But at lower levels, foundations and remains of buildings begin to emerge from the murk below.

During my lunch break, the wind picks up. It stays relatively warm, but it's blowing twenty, making the crossing to the Flagstaff Hut at Maine Huts and Trails a challenge in the sharp, breaking waves that push the boat off course. By the time I reach the hut, I'm ready to be done.

I haul the boat up the dock, and rest it upside-down under a tree next to another canoe. I make my way to the hut, put down the pack and remove my shoes at the front door.

As I walk in, a chipper young man sporting a scruffy black beard says, "You must be John Connelly."

This is the first time I'm not surprised to hear that. I made a reservation. I'm a founding board member of Maine Huts and Trails, and it was well known that I would be spending a night on my way through. I planned to spend two nights, but when I hear that there is a group of thirty elementary school kids coming in the next day, I get up early and hightail it out of there. Is all this time alone making me antisocial? I think not. Any reasonable person would have bolted. Right?

My timing is perfect. The Dead River below Flagstaff Lake sees scheduled recreational whitewater flow releases a dozen times a year. Whitewater paddlers of all stripes descend upon the Dead for these flows, as do the local whitewater rafting outfitters. I guide rafts occasionally for Northern Outdoors, based in The Forks, where the Kennebec and Dead Rivers meet, hence the name. I think it would be awesome to take a break from paddling to guide a Class III-IV, fifteen-mile, 7,000 cubic feet per second, high water rafting trip down the Dead

The Trail follows the Dead River below Flagstaff Lake, portages forty-foot Grand Falls, and then hangs a sharp left, ascending Spencer Stream to Little Spencer Stream to Spencer Lake. From there, portaging to the Moose River watershed will eventually take me to Moosehead Lake. The spot where this sharp left up Spencer Stream occurs is where the raft groups put-in for the Dead river trips. Northern Outdoors sends a pickup truck to retrieve me and my gear, and plants me in one of their cabins at the adventure resort. The resort happens to be home of the Kennebec River Brewing Company. How will I cope?

I subject myself to Magic Hole India Pale Ales in the lodge's jacuzzi and chat with friends, awaiting Nicole's arrival. She's on time. We have dinner, and in preparation for a big day on the river, a good night's sleep.

Couldn't ask for better: it's a warm, bluebird day and I am high water rafting with Nicole. The guests in my raft are feeling the effects of last night's bachelor party. Thankfully, these guys are no strangers to the gym. They spring into action on command and do everything I ask them to do. Between paddling efforts, they sit silently and suffer. I've had rowdy crews who don't listen to anything I say. I've even had mutinies. This is perfect.

Back at the lodge, along with 120 others, we enjoy the the day's raft trip video, complete with swimmers and rescue ropes flying. None of the carnage is mine. With a fun, long day behind us, another dinner at the lodge, a few beers with friends and a sound night's sleep is in order.

The following day, Nicole heads back to the real world and I'm transported back to the point where I was picked up at the mouth of Spencer Stream. I alternate between paddling and tracking upstream in a water course that, in places, is not much wider than the boat is long. I feel the barometer falling and the temperature dropping. By nighttime, while setting up my shelter on Fish Pond, it once again spits snow that begins to accumulate on brown grasses and green pine boughs. I make dinner in the vestibule of the tent to stay warm and dry. I am pretty confident that last night was much better.

The morning's long portage into the Moose River is over a network of gravel logging roads. When I am almost to the river, two pickups loaded with canoes approach. The first one stops and a genial older couple ask me what the heck I'm doing out there with a backpack, towing a canoe on wheels. I tell them my story.

Suitably impressed, the woman says, "Then you could use some cookies."

I gratefully accept the unopened package of Pepperidge Farms Milano Cookies. They would propel me through the rest of my day. The truck disappears around the bend, and there I stand with a handful of cookies. The next truck stops. After a similar explanation of what I'm doing, the passenger in front leans forward and lifts his sunglasses.

"Are you John Connelly?" he says.

I'm not sure what to do with this and I'm pretty sure my mouth just fell open. We are in the middle of nowhere. What are the chances? I confirm and he refreshes my memory.

"It's Howard, John. I was in the Maine senate. We knew each other in the eighties." He turns to the driver. "This guy can really paddle a canoe. I mean, really paddle one."

I'm a little embarrassed and still amazed by all these coincidences. But it sure is cool.

Finally, I reach the Moose River, and after a few quiet miles of paddling, I camp at Attean Falls. It's cold, but with virtually no wind.

The campsite is like a postcard: winding river flanked by pines and grass with rock covered shores. I'll paddle the falls first thing in the morning and check off another twenty or so miles.

I awake to wind, wind, and more wind from the northwest. It persists, as I do battle across the lakes of the Moose River system, making for a long day. After portaging the gnarly rapid at Demo Road, the last section of the Moose to Little Brassua Lake puts a smile on my face with its continuous, easily read whitewater. At the foot of the rapids emptying into Little Brassua Lake I find a perfect campsite. The moon casts shadows of white pines across a washboard of sparkling water and loons call me out for a nighttime paddle. Sometimes sleep is overrated.

In the soft morning light, eagles fish, ducks chatter, and a pair of geese splash to a halt across the cove while a gentle mist rises from the lake's surface. It's clear that the wind has blown itself out and won't return anytime soon. I have major lake crossings for the next two days and it looks to be glassy-water perfect.

Across Little Brassua into Brassua Lake, I portage around the dam and paddle down the last moving section of the Moose River into Moosehead Lake. When I owned one of the state's first whitewater rafting companies, I lived on this twenty-mile wide, nearly forty-mile-long lake. For almost twenty years, I got to know how fickle it can be. One minute calm; the next minute threatening to take your life. Today, it looks like the gods are smiling on me.

Tonight will be the last roof over my head until Fort Kent. It's a rustic, lakeside cabin at The Birches Resort in Rockwood, owned by John Willard, a friend of ours. It's preseason, so the restaurant and bar aren't yet open. I borrow an employee's pickup to run up to the local pub for lunch, a beer, and a few snacks, as I'm running low. This is our tenth wedding anniversary but Nicole can't make the trip to join me because of a business obligation. We'll have to make it up somehow. Until now, Nicole has been bringing my reprovisions. This time she mailed them to The Birches for me to collect. It will be five days before I see another open store, so I need the delivery. It hasn't arrived.

A dinner invitation with John, his wife, daughter, and a couple of their friends is eagerly accepted. I didn't expect martinis overlooking the lake, a delicious meal and such good company. I explain to John the need to receive my care package, and he tells me not to worry. His cousin works at the post office. If the package is there, he'll get it. If he can't get it before I leave, he'll fly his float plane up the lake and deliver it to me. I have good friends.

I'm just about packed up and ready to get on the water when one of The Birches staff walks over and hands me my package. Just in the knick of time. Nicole comes through again.

For the twenty-mile paddle to its end at Northeast Carry, the only ripples on Moosehead are from the wake of the canoe and my paddle strokes. Vertigo is an issue. The sky and water meld on the horizon, making for a spatial relationship problem solved only by scanning the shoreline or looking at the wake from the bow. This is a day to remember.

The portage at Northeast Carry takes me to the Penobscot River watershed and its Upper West Branch. I pass by Thoreau Island, where the famous writer camped on a similar journey. Had the lake been rougher and paddling it taken longer, I had planned to camp here and immerse myself in Thoreau history and his writings, but I'm ahead of schedule so I keep going.

Teardrop shaped, Big Island has a campsite at its downstream end. Over the years, I've paddled this river three times and this has always been my favorite campsite. In wishbone fashion, the river flows down both sides of the island and disappears downstream. I'm surrounded on three sides by fast moving water. Not a blackfly or mosquito in sight to suck me dry. A little slice of heaven.

Paddling gear is prone to reeking in very short order, especially when stewing in sweat under a hermetically sealed dry suit. The resulting stench may help repel intruders from camp, but there are those whose company I want to welcome. I make an effort to thoroughly dry my gear at day's end and I use a natural, unscented deodorant. Unscented, because blackflies are drawn to anything with the slightest perfume and I mean *slightest.* I have borne witness to this and it's not pretty. Stink or get eaten alive? Thankfully, there's the unscented option.

The following afternoon, I arrive at Chesuncook Village, which marks the end of the Upper West Branch of the Penobscot River and the beginning of a twenty-mile lake created by yet another dam, Ripogenus. Chesuncook is a remote, extinct logging town, now with a few camps, an inn and a small store. I'm hoping to pick up a treat at the store but it's closed. I spot four men on the porch of a nearby camp fiddling with their fishing gear. It's primetime for catching landlocked salmon on the surface of the lake before warm water drives them deep. I head over for a chat.

A short way into asking if the store is due to open, I'm stopped and asked if I'd like lunch and a beer. The next hour is spent learning about how the men came to own the camp, where they are from, and a little history about Chesuncook Village, the log drives, and the jobs lost when the paper industry left the region. Most intriguing is the discussion about the raft trips they went on below the dam through Ripogenus Gorge, the Cribworks Rapid, and the miles below at the foot of Mount Katahdin. I dig deeper.

They say their rafting years were during the eighties. I ask them about the rafting company they used. They've forgotten the name, but remember all the details: orange rafts, white helmets and based in Greenville, on Moosehead Lake. Rhetorically, I ask if it was Eastern River Expeditions. I smile.

A fresh bite of ham and cheese in his cheek, the man across the table says, "Hey, aren't you the guy who owned the company?"

This isn't exactly, "Are you John Connelly?" but about as close as it gets. I hope my memory is as good when I'm his age. These are great guys.

Pushing two Coors Lites into my hands, they wish me luck. I head back to the canoe, feeling an urgency to get going. This stop puts in question where I will end my day, but I convince myself to push hard and hope to make the Allagash Wilderness Waterway by dark.

The most notorious portage of the entire Northern Forest Canoe Trail is the Mud Pond Carry. It's under two miles but includes blowdowns across the path and up-to-waist-deep slogging in muddy water, being jabbed with the sharp ends of sticks chewed off by resident beavers. I quickly scout the trail. It is not immediately apparent that there is a trail at all. It looks more like a tiny runoff stream flowing between rocks and over tree roots.

No way I'm making it in one trip. The blowdowns, sketchy footing, and waist deep muck promised at the far end, make navigating with a loaded pack and canoe overhead near to impossible. If I hustle, I can get this done pretty quickly. I'm glad I have trekking poles.

First trip is with the canoe because I know it will be the most frustrating. I'm right. I never fall down, but saving myself from lost balance is exhausting. Ducking through downed logs and tree branches while stepping through underwater rocks, roots and mud with a canoe over my head is awkward at best. I arrive at the deep-water section of the trail and think about getting in the canoe and paddling. How bad can it be?

I press on, canoe overhead, with the waterline topping my waist and heading for my chest. The dry bibs protect me from the leeches, but if it gets any deeper, they will fill up with this bog water. If I weren't wearing hightop paddling boots, I'm sure my footwear would be sucked off in the muck below. Submerged sticks and logs hamper progress and I wonder if being on top of the canoe, instead of under it, might have been the smarter choice.

I drop the canoe at Mud Pond and slog back through the churned-up waters to retrieve the pack. Just a few yards to my right, I hear a pair of deer bounding away, and a beaver slaps its tail in objection to my intrusion. Little black-winged gnats begin to swarm around my head and sweat drips off my nose. I'm looking forward to having this carry behind me.

The put-in on Mud Pond is a floating hummock that threatens to devour me with every weight-bearing step. I scurry quickly to get the boat afloat and throw myself aboard. The outflow from the pond consists of tight, zig-zagging, rocky rapids carrying just enough water to save me from another portage. They eventually open up into Mud Cove on Chamberlain Lake as night approaches. I'm officially in the Allagash Wilderness Waterway. The blackflies know it.

If I inhale, I'll choke on these things, and I don my no-see-um head net. It saves my life. I've seen horrendous blackflies in my time, but this is spectacular. No way am I making camp while these guys are still out. I resolve to paddle up the lake until after dark, when union rules require the little bastards to punch out for the day.

The sun sets over the bow of the canoe. Directly behind, the moon rises over Baxter State Park and the Mount Katahdin massif, silhouetted magnificently above Chamberlain Lake. Truly magical.

After a sound sleep, I find myself trying to brush my teeth under the head net in an ongoing battle with the flies. One fly looks odd to me. I realize he's on the wrong side of the netting. I give him a squeeze to ruin his day and am squirted with my own blood. He already got me.

Head net in place, I paddle toward the middle of the lake to shake the black cloud of flies obscuring the sun's rays. It works, for the most part.

It will take me just three days to paddle the ninety miles of Allagash Wilderness Waterway. My big day is forty-four-and-a-half miles but, even at this fast pace, I manage to appreciate every moment along the way.

At Churchill Dam, I camp for the night to await the morning river flow release that makes the several miles of rapids below the dam possible to run. I'm chatting with a ranger at the dam, when a pickup pulls in. An oddly familiar man in a tan Carhartt jacket steps out, ambles over and starts asking me questions about my logo'd canoe. He stops in mid-sentence.

"Hey, you're John Connelly," he says.

I'm floored.

"Years ago, I used to compete in canoe races that you sponsored. I've been following you on Facebook. How've ya been?"

We chat for twenty-or-so minutes. He wishes me good luck, and I tell him I'm glad he stopped. Then off he goes in a gray cloud of logging road dust.

The Allagash Wilderness Waterway has a unique perk not often found on remote rivers. For a mere fifteen dollars, paddlers can pay to have the ranger shuttle their gear to the end of Chase Rapid, the longest and most consequential of the river's whitewater. This makes for lightweight boats and easier maneuvering, and likely results in the rangers dealing with fewer wrecks on the river. While I've taken advantage of this service in the past, I view it as cheating on this particular trip. I plan to run the rapids fully loaded with no help from the outside world.

The ranger will crack open the dam mid-morning, so I enjoy a leisurely morning of coffee, oatmeal and packing. I don't want to jump on the river right after the dam is opened, because I don't want to catch up to, and pass, the front end of the flow. That would put me on low, slow water, dodging rocks. Not as much fun at all. One canoe puts in well ahead of me, not long after the flow begins. They might find out that they should have waited.

After an hour of water heads downstream in front of me, off I go. The Class II rapids are continuous and fun but I have to pay attention and look way ahead, especially with a loaded canoe. I wouldn't be the first to have a yard sale on this stretch. Five miles downstream, I pass the pair of canoeists who left in front of me. They are both soaked and they seem to be arguing. Looks like their run hasn't gone as smoothly as mine.

Round Pond has a ranger's camp at its midpoint. I spot the ranger working on her canoe. I stop and strike up a conversation. As many conversations go, we explore common themes and experiences to find a connection. She mentions having done a lot to get her daughter into the outdoors; to have her feel the love for it that she does. She talks about taking her on raft trips and that she used to be a guide. In mid-sentence, she abruptly stops, squints hard, and looks me up and down.

"You're John Connelly, aren't you?" she says.

I nod, but not in disbelief. I'm beyond that.

"I used to work for you as a raft guide on the Kennebec and Penobscot, back in the eighties!"

In that instant, I recognize her and could even picture the color of lifejacket and helmet she wore. It occurs to me that, if I ever have to run from the law or want to fade into anonymity, I can never retreat to the woods and waters.

I make a point of not missing the eddy on the right bank above the famed Allagash Falls. These are a forty-foot, spectacularly violent, steep cascade roaring through a gray, granite gorge, flanked by towering white pines. Half of the portage is marginally wheelable, but the rest is impossible. It's short enough that I hoof it in two trips, then have lunch next to five-foot high banks of snow left on the riverside by the recent winter. A powerful place, and the view is impressive.

A few miles more and I have completed the Allagash Wilderness Waterway. I think back to my last time here. It was with Nicole and was a hot, cloudless July day. Moose were everywhere in the cool river water seeking relief from the heat, and dining on water grasses. Today is just as clear, but twenty degrees cooler and not a moose to be seen. Bald eagles are abundant and I spook a whitetail deer as I round the last bend before the quaint settlement of Allagash Village, which marks the end of the Waterway.

Passing beneath the first paved road bridge I've seen in a week, I join the Saint John River for the rest of its journey to the Bay of Fundy. Many times the width of the Allagash, it carries greater flow. The rapids are much pushier, requiring more attention. A few miles more and I spot a large grassy field with picnic tables overlooking the river on the right. It's Pelletier's Campground and shuttle service, my overnight stop.

I pull the canoe high on the bank, turn it over for its night of rest, and shoulder my pack. I climb the bank, drop the pack by a campsite, and head to the office to check-in. There are no signs of life anywhere. Not surprising; it's still pre-season.

I raid the convenience store next door. A six pack of IPA, two tuna and two chicken salad sandwiches, and a fudge brownie the size of a cinder block accompany me to the site where I choose to make my camp. In the field, there are no insects and in the fading, rose-colored light, I reach Nicole by phone for the first time in five days. So good to hear her voice.

I'm up with the sun and return to the convenience store for four breakfast sandwiches and another fudge brownie. Back at the site overlooking the river, a white long-bed GMC pickup truck descends the drive. It's Norman L'Italien, the owner of the campground and shuttle service. We quickly connect, as I had hired him to run my shuttle for the Allagash Wilderness Waterway just two years ago. The key thing that jogs his memory is that on one of the gravel logging roads, his shuttle driver destroyed the sidewall of a tire on our Honda Element. He had to get it replaced before I got off the river, so he had to drive over 200 miles from Saint Francis to Bangor, Maine to find a match.

It cost me $170.00 for the replacement tire, but Norman had seven hours of driving. Now that's customer service. Probably not his happiest memory. I wonder why I brought that up.

While I pack up, we chat about how the season's campground and shuttle reservations are looking and lament the lack of snowpack or appreciable spring rain. Norman refuses payment for the site, wishes me well, and says he hopes to see me back on the Allagash again.

This is my last day on the Northern Forest Canoe Trail. Shadows grow long as I glide beneath the International Bridge between the United States and Canada at Fort Kent, Maine. The bridge marks Mile 2,369 of US Route One, Mile zero being in Key West, Florida. Now I've been to both ends. I'm sure that US Customs is watching. As I approach the boat ramp where I'll take out, I see an armed border patrol agent leaning against the front of his patrol car. I nudge the bow ashore.

"I'll bet you're here for me, aren't you?" I say.

"How'd you guess?" he laughs.

Routine check behind me, I ask the officer if he'll take my picture in front of the Northern Forest Canoe Trail sign next to the parking lot, marking completion of the Trail at its Eastern Terminus. He's delighted. I've officially completed through-paddling the 740-mile-longTrail, which is merely the first leg of a much longer journey. I drag the canoe to the only motel in town, then it's time to head to the Swamp Buck Pub for a pile of protein and some lubrication to celebrate.

Sixty degrees and sunny, it's a perfect morning to hit the Saint John River and crank out some blissful miles. I park the canoe in front of a grocery store. Inside, incredulous looks follow me as I peruse the aisles to stock up on Clif Bars and other snacks. I'm eyeballed by a man in a well-worn leather biker's jacket adorned with Prisoner of War emblems and American flags. He leans on his cane, waiting for me to queue up at the register. I know the first question before it's asked.

"What are you up to that you're dressed like that?"

I give him a brief explanation while inching forward, hoping that the line moves more quickly. With his free hand, he nudges up the brim of his blue US Veteran ball cap for a better look.

"You came from where and you're going where?"

The line ratchets forward and I'm number one. As I place my items on the belt, the veteran works his way down to the bagging area of the adjacent closed checkout lane and is waiting for me. While paying, I give him the longer version.

I explain: Old Forge, New York in the Adirondacks, down the Saint John, Bay of Fundy and coast of Maine to Kittery; 1500 miles and I'm thinking seventy-five days. Now the store's other shoppers have stopped what they were doing and are looking and listening.

His gray beard is just long enough to twist with his fingers, signaling deep thought. He laments that he always wanted to take a long canoe trip, but never did it. I tell him that it's not too late. He ponders that a second while I stuff snacks in my dry bag and eyeball the exit. His eyes brighten.

"I suppose you're right," he says, smiling like he'd just been given a gift.

"If you really want to do it, Friend, just get out there and make it happen," I say. "And thank you for your service, sir."

As I drag the canoe down the street toward the boat ramp, I'm hopeful that he'll act on it. Maybe I've inspired him to realize that dream of his. I'd like to think so.

CHAPTER EIGHT

— Wolastog: The Good and Beautiful River —

Second only to the Susquehanna River, the Saint John, originally named *Wolastog* by the Maliseet people, is the longest river between the Saint Lawrence and Mississippi Rivers. For millennia, aboriginal people have canoed its length and its tributaries for trade, hunting and fishing, and more recently for recreation. Or so you would imagine. But do you think I could find a canoeing guidebook?

It's been a challenge to get any details about my route down the Saint John River below Fort Kent, Maine from a paddler's perspective. Unable to find a guidebook or any outfitters, I assume that it doesn't see much canoe or kayak traffic. There are few, if any, commercial campgrounds and no approved campsites for boaters along the river. Using Google Earth, I've located and way-pointed potential stealth camping sites along the way. At least I'm not going into it blind. It's always important to have options.

I hear it in her voice over the phone and I am eager, too. It's been ten long days since seeing Nicole back in The Forks for the rafting trip. In only two days I will be meeting her in Grand Falls, New Brunswick for more supplies and to trade this trusty canoe for my kayak, to complete the final seven hundred miles.

Not a cloud, no wind and seventy degrees. Perfect. From this point, I need to be careful to stay on the United States' half of the river unless I want to create an international incident. As I paddle, it feels as if I'm being watched by some unseen Homeland Security aerial surveillance, but it's probably just in my head. Or is it?

Fort Kent is now in my rearview mirror and I'm curious about this next section of river the Canadians call Les Rapides. However, at today's lower water level there are no rapids. There are quick water channels winding around polished granite ledges as the river slowly bends. A bald eagle alights on a pine branch sixty feet above me to scope out the fishing situation. Below here, the river is wide and flat with few ripples. There are occasional islands, some large enough to be actively farmed or grazed, and river-wide gravel bars provide multiple choice, downstream Vs of swift water.

I hear the low thrumming of diesel engines idling at Canadian National Railway's yard on river left. Interestingly, there are no visible signs of life down on the river as I pass unseen through the industrial landscape of Madawaska, Maine on my right and Edmundston, New Brunswick on my left. A bit further on, the developed world unfolds. The mill operations of the Twin Rivers Paper Company occupy both sides of the river in a unique arrangement where the same company operates on both sides of the border. The Edmundston pulp mill delivers bleached, softwood sulphite and bleached, groundwood pulp to the Madawaska paper mill through a giant conduit that soars across the river ninety-or-so feet high. The pulp from Canada is used for the manufacture of specialized packaging and lightweight, specialty papers. I crane my neck in awe as I paddle beneath the humming pipe.

Despite so many people living and working on both sides of the river, the waterfront is oddly stark and uninviting. I'm hoping to find a portable toilet but there are no parks or any other likely spots for a pit stop. Downstream of Madawaska, I pull up at the only boat ramp I've seen since Fort Kent. With nobody in sight, I secure the boat on the bank and find a bush. It seems that the river is little used for recreation. It makes me wonder if having the international border run down the middle of the river complicates things for would-be river users. I push on, spooking a large flock of Canada geese as I round the next bend between the US shore and a mid-stream Canadian island thick with pines and budding hardwoods.

Canadian National Railway tracks dominate the river left bank. Otherwise, both banks host barren fields for crops yet to surface, bordered by scant forest. There's no sound of tractors tilling the land or, for that matter, any sound at all, except from a raft of a dozen ducks ahead chattering their annoyance at my approach. In fact, the air feels dead. I know why. The barometer is plummeting.

I scan the western sky above the tree line. Only the very top of an anvil-shaped black cloud is visible. Quickly, I refer to my iPad navigation screen, looking for the next town where I can seek shelter. I could plan on hunkering down under the cover of shoreline trees somewhere, but I'd be in for a soaking, and trees often get struck by lightning. A human-made shelter with a lightning rod would be better if I can find one.

At this point, I am open to the idea of suffering the consequences of seeking civilized safety on the Canadian side. Fortunately, the nearest town on either side is Grand Isle, Maine, about four miles downstream. I look back to the horizon. Now I can see the entire anvil and hear the first rumble of distant thunder. The storm is moving fast. In two strokes, I hit race pace and paddle like my life depends upon it. It's going to be close.

The calm before the storm is ominous and eerie. Thunder is louder, the reports come only seconds apart, and I can see the occasional flash of lightning out of my peripheral vision. I am grateful to see a flat-bottomed Johnboat being cranked out of the water onto a trailer at a ramp by the end of the next straightaway. That has to be Grand Isle. I pick up the pace, but have already hit maximum hull speed for the canoe, so back off to avoid wasting energy.

Everything turns dark, as if a black cloak has been tossed over the sun. No longer are ducks or songbirds flittering anxiously about. Everyone has sought shelter. The smart ones, anyway. The looming storm of Armageddon-like proportions is about to hit. I make it to the concrete ramp and pull ashore through the weeds next to it.

Behind their sixteen-foot aluminum outboard boat, now on its trailer, three men hurriedly rinse their harvest of fiddleheads, delectable wild succulent ferns picked only in spring before they unfurl their fronds. They resemble the tightly curled scroll at the end of a violin, hence the name, fiddlehead. I like mine steamed, dressed with vinegar.

The men are working as frantically as I am to get packed up and out of here. They only need to make it to the cab of their pickup truck, but I have nowhere to go.

"Where's the nearest motel or place to get a room?" I ask, while tossing everything onto the parking lot to get the canoe on its cart.

Without looking up from hefting a dripping basket of greens into the bed of the pickup, one of the clean-shaven, middle-aged men, this one in a Red Sox sweatshirt, says, "There's nothing within miles of here." He looks at the sky, then me, climbs into the truck and slams the door.

"How about a campground?" I ask one of the other guys as I snug the straps of the cart around the canoe, then throw my pack straps over my shoulders hopeful for something positive.

"There's a campground two miles north. But they're not open and you're not going to make it," says the last man to board the truck, pointing to the roiling black sky. The door slams and off they go up the hill and out of sight.

"That's just great."

The first gusts of warm, moisture laden wind brush my face as I round the bend at the top of the boat ramp hill. To my left is a small, well-kept, white house with veranda. On the deck is a woman taking a video of the approaching maelstrom. This sure is a big one if she is filming its approach. I need shelter, and quick. And not two miles up the road.

Maybe I can get lucky. I shoot her a big smile and head straight toward her.

"You got back just in time!" she calls out to me.

"I'm not getting back. I'm passing through. Is there a campground nearby?" I shout over the growling sky, praying she'll allow me to use her yard.

"You're passing through?" she says, in disbelief. I get a sense that there aren't a lot of passersby on the river.

"Yes, I'm on a big trip. My name is John Connelly. I'm from Falmouth, Maine."

"My name is Liz," she says. Then the most astounding thing happens.

"You're not going anywhere. In ten minutes, you'll be having dinner with me and my husband at our kitchen table and you'll be spending the night in our gazebo overlooking the river. Now let's get you set up. This thing's about to hit!" she shouts.

Just in time, another Trail Angel.

There's no time to take the boat off the cart. I toss my gear into the gazebo, and cable the canoe to the railing just in case. Can't let it get blown to Canada. Dodging the first penny-size droplets pounding the earth, I bolt through their back door to safety. As promised, ten minutes after Liz's offer, the three of us are saying grace at the kitchen table. A pile of mac and cheese with my name on it sits before me. The lights flicker and all hell breaks loose.

One of the most violet thunderstorms in my memory, I'll be amazed if this doesn't spawn tornadoes. It's awkward trying to have a *Getting to Know You* conversation and review Liz's portfolio of bald eagle images, while Mother Nature so boisterously demands our attention. A clap of thunder outside the front door seems to lift the house a couple of inches and drop it. The framed eagle on the kitchen wall tilts left and dishes rattle in cabinets. Everyone's eyes dart toward the door to make sure it's still there. The lights flicker off, but we can still see. The whole interior is illuminated by a Pink Floyd laser light show, refracted through thick sheets of rain over glass. The lights flicker back on, but the windows keep flashing wildly. Repeated cracks of thunder are deafening and the unspoken thought on everyone's mind is clear on our faces. Are we going to get hit? Maybe it's time to pray again.

Twenty-five minutes after the storm began, the outside air is still once more. Rays of sunshine pierce the overcast, and the evening begins with the day's last gasp of light. Whitecaps on the river have smoothed and the first birds can be seen plying the sky, seeming to scout for storm damage while diving for newly emerged flying insects. On my way to the gazebo I notice at least five gallons of water in the canoe. It would be great if the storm pumps the river up, but I'm sure it was too localized to have much effect.

After breakfast with my two new friends, I dump the water out of the canoe, slide on my pack and head to the boat ramp. I will be forever grateful to these folks for taking me in when I needed it most.

We exchange information and vow to stay in touch.

If ever you're back in the neighborhood...

If you're ever in the Portland area...

I would enjoy spending more time getting to know them, but I need to cross the border and make Grand Falls, New Brunswick, before dark. Last night, I reserved a motel room by phone for me and Nicole. Can't wait.

I was told about the military fortress-like US Customs facility in Van Buren, Maine. As I pass beneath a railroad bridge, I see a gate crowned with razor wire across the tracks on the U.S. side. Approaching the road bridge spanning the river between Van Buren and the Canadian Customs facility in Saint Leonard, New Brunswick, I see a dock on our side, but only a steep embankment to the road on the Canadian side. Well downstream of the border crossing there is a boat ramp on that side but I'm hesitant to paddle by Canadian customs toward the distant ramp, so stop in to chat with the American border patrol.

They may have a dock, but they're not set up for visitors coming off the river. I find myself trudging through town in dry bibs and a pfd to walk up to Customs using the auto road. Pulling up to the window on foot, I receive an incredulous look from the agent and am "invited" inside. It's pretty much an interrogation but I'm not surprised. I'm certainly an oddity.

"I don't even have to be stopping here to talk to you guys," I say. "I haven't been to Canada, so I'm not re-entering the country. I want to enter Canada, but they don't have a dock and I'm unsure how to approach them. I don't want to surprise them by climbing over the river bank in paddling gear wearing a pfd bristling with radios and a knife."

After a grilling and a check of my passport, their demeanor changes and one of the agents volunteers to give the Canadian officers across the river a call to let them know I'm coming. That should work. Off I go.

I ferry across the river, haul the canoe high out of the water, scale the embankment, and walk in. I didn't expect them to ask, *Are you John Connelly?* but I did expect them to know I was coming. Neither of the two officers processing my entry into the country knew of a heads-up by phone from the other side. Oh well.

Another nine-or-so miles downstream is the city of Grand Falls. Named after an actual falls, this is a definite portage. There's a concrete dam built atop a tall waterfall, which cascades sixty feet into the narrow gorge below. I ask one of the officers about a take-out above the falls. I want to be able to recognize it in plenty of time.

"You'll pass beneath a bridge and the marina will be on your left. It's well above the falls. There's a restaurant and bar there," he says.

I perk up and am eager to get back on the water.

Five miles downstream, a man is making preseason preparations to his pontoon boat, obviously used for tourist excursions on the river. I pull alongside to ask how much further to the marina. He has a swoosh of black grease across his cheek, his corrugated skin shows the effects of weather, and his smile is warm. His English, spoken with a thick French accent, is impeccable. He tells me he's recently retired and runs cruises to the gorge and back. I tell him that I plan to take out at the marina, and use the canoe cart to hike the mile and a half back up the road to the motel. I ask him if I need to go via the marina, or if there's a trail or road from the river that goes directly up to the motel to avoid backtracking.

"The marina is your best bet. I can pick you up with my truck and take you to your motel," he says.

I gratefully decline and give my usual explanation. He is fascinated. He reaches into his shirt pocket, passes me his business card, then takes it back to write his cell phone number.

"If you need anything at all while you are in New Brunswick, not just Grand Falls, but anywhere, I will come help you. It's preseason, I'm retired and have nothing but time. It's no problem," he says.

I thank him, humbled by his generosity. My faith in humanity is getting a much-needed boost on this trip. I stroke toward the falls.

I haul up on the marina's sand beach, pull the canoe next to a row of bushes, and climb the hill for a beer at the bar. It's a Moosehead. Not usually my favorite, but it's been living in ice and tastes exquisite. The bartender asks about my paddling trip as a regular customer walks in. I tell the story, including that I'm staying in the motel up the road. The customer asks me if I'd like a ride. I decline and tell him why. He says there are several ways to get to the motel and asks if I'd like to go on a scouting ride to pick the best route for the hike. I accept. Fifteen minutes later I'm back at the canoe and am clear about my route. What nice people.

As I put the canoe on its cart, I realize that I'm not getting back in it. Nicole is bringing my kayak and I'm paddling that from here. It's a bittersweet moment. I feel a twinge. I flash back to the whitewater; the portages; plying our wake across mirrored surfaces; the violent storms. I've grown fond of this canoe. We've built a bond. Snap out of it, John. You're not having a relationship with a canoe.

CHAPTER NINE

— The Royal Canadian Mounted Police —

I walk along narrow neighborhood streets lined with modest single-family homes and white picket fences, to a long stretch of busy, two lane road with tractor-trailer trucks whizzing by. The mile-and-a-half dragging the canoe seems like it's all uphill and I'm glad when it's over. Still in paddling clothes, drenched in sweat, I check-in to the Quality Inn on the Trans-Canada Highway. I cable the canoe to the awning post by the parking space in front of my door. I have only one more item to shuttle into the room, when the door slams shut behind me. The key's on the bureau. Crap.

I go back to the office and confess. With another key, I head back to my room. Then things get interesting.

I'm fifty feet from the room when a Royal Canadian Mounted Police cruiser wheels in from the Trans-Canada Highway, coming to a sliding stop behind my canoe, as if to block it in and keep it from escaping. The officer springs from the driver's door with one hand on his gun. With the free hand, he points his finger at the man in paddling clothes standing in the parking lot with a room key in his hand.

"French or English?" he shouts.

"English. I'm American," I say, wide-eyed.

"Is that your canoe?" he yells, gun hand twitching.

My mind races, struggling against the wise guy in my head. My knee-jerk is to say, *What canoe? Nope, not mine,* but that could put me behind bars.

"Yes. That's my canoe," I say. *You idiot.*

He sprints over to me. From three feet away, he demands my identification.

"My passport is in my room," I say.

"I can cuff you and throw you in the back of the cruiser."

"Do what you want with me, Officer, but I'm not going anywhere."

"Then I'm confining you to your room."

I've heard that before, but it's been a while and I think, *Well, okay, Dad.* I open the room, grab my dry bag, and hand him my passport.

"Don't you go anywhere," he says.

"Don't worry, I'm not going anywhere."

Ten minutes later, he returns. I've taken the opportunity to change into dry clothes. He opens the door, steps in, hand on his gun, clearly confrontational. I'm confused.

"There is no record of you having entered the country," he barks.

"What? You're kidding," I say. Clearly, he's not.

I spend the next five minutes giving him the detailed account of stopping at U.S. Customs to ask about approaching the Canadians who didn't have a dock; US agents calling over to let the Canadian side know I'm coming; and my conversation about finding the marina.

"Don't go anywhere," he says, closing the door behind him.

Another ten minutes grind by and the door opens. His hand is not on his gun this time.

He hands me my passport.

"You're in the country legally. Have a nice visit," he says, and turns to walk away.

"Hey, what's this all about?" I ask.

"There's an all points bulletin out for all of law enforcement in the area with a report of someone trying to jump the border by canoe," he says, over his shoulder.

Watching him leave, I realize that driving by on the Trans-Canada Highway, he saw the canoe parked in front of my room, cabled to a post, and thought he cracked the case. I chuckle at how dumb he thinks this fugitive must be. Oh, how I wish he had cuffed me and thrown me in the back of his cruiser. It would have made for a much richer story.

CHAPTER TEN

— Ground Support —

There's a knock at the door. Dripping wet from a much-needed hose-down, I wrap a towel around my waist and sprint toward the door. Through a gap in the curtains, I see the Jeep with my bright yellow logo'd kayak on top. It's my incomparable wife. I yank the door open, and she charges in. The towel drops.

Nicole spends the next four nights and three days burning some precious vacation time, rooting for me, and taking stills and videos of my grimacing face grinding my way down the Saint John River.

In the kayak, my average speed will pick up at least one mile per hour or so versus the speed of my beloved canoe, and it won't be as dramatically affected by the wind. I'm looking forward to the next seven hundred miles.

Nicole sees me off at the Grand Falls hydroelectric generating facility below the narrow granite gorge, which lies beneath the falls. The bank is muddy, so I'm challenged to get afloat and into the boat without introducing a couple of pounds of brown, cement-like goo into my traveling space. I manage by sitting in the kayak and draping my feet overboard for a thorough rinse. I pull my feet inside, extend them to the foot braces, secure the sprayskirt around the flange of the cockpit to keep the boat dry, and tell Nicole I will see her downstream. Her plan for the next couple of days is to find places to intercept me and take photos, but also to find us suitable lodging nearby, at the end of each day's paddle.

Nicole videos my departure and will spend the next couple of hours scouting out a place to stay about twenty-four miles downstream in Perth-Andover. She'll be looking for a hot tub and the best taps around. Now *that's* ground support.

She watches as I round the first bend and dip out of sight. This time, when I pull away and leave her on the bank waving, I am not sad at all, but excited about what lies ahead.

When researching the river on Google Earth, I saw heavy current and rapids below this point. This morning, two staffers at the Visitor's Center told me the river was so deep for miles below the power station, that the flow was buffered and there was no whitewater.

I remember that the Google Earth view of the rapids didn't look difficult, so I'll take my chances. Catching the downstream momentum of the flow, I approach what looks like a horizon line. My pulse quickens.

The staffers at the Visitor's Center were wrong. This flow has to be over ten thousand cubic feet per second, and there are definitely rapids with three-to-five-foot standing waves, but no visible granite between the shores. At least they were right about it being deep.

I taste the first couple of rapids and integrate into the river's flow and rhythms. I relax. Each rapid is easy to read on the fly and I sense that the consistent geology and topography won't throw something unexpected at me, like a big drop or technical rapid. For miles, I fly down the river at race pace, the scenery a blur. This is the most fun I've had since Chase Rapids on the Allagash.

I paddle past the Maliseet Indian Reservation on river left where the Tobique River's flow joins the Saint John and see my fifth bald eagle of the day. Somehow this sighting has more significance with the backdrop of the Native American community.

Nicole meets me at a park on river right in Perth-Andover. It has been a relatively short day, paddling on high water at a blistering pace. More time to spend with Nicole. She can't wait to show me where we're staying. We cross the river, follow a narrow drive up a hill, around a corner, through a wrought iron gate, and there it is. A castle.

A serious stone castle: heavy, dark wood front doors with iron hinges; ivy crawling up the walls; majestic trees and carefully manicured budding gardens. Atop is a medieval stone tower. All that is missing is

Rapunzel throwing down her hair from an open window. Nicole jumps from the car and extracts me.

"You're gonna love this!" she says. Grabbing me by the hand, she pulls me through the front door.

Inside, it looks and feels like a castle alright, and the fragrance of roasting vegetables fills the air. To our right is a formal dining room with dark hardwood furniture, sparkling goblets and shiny silverware settings. Nicole whisks me past the small mahogany bar, and points out the stairs to our room on the left. She drags me down a hallway into a new building, and swings open the door. There before me is a heated swimming pool with a slide. Beyond it, by a picture window, is a ten-person jacuzzi.

"I think we're the only ones here," she says.

She's right. I love it.

In the morning, we decide to sample local cuisine outside the castle. Breakfast is at a riverside café with a European vibe. The meal is delicious, so we order sandwiches to go for our lunch and enjoy a second cup of coffee while we wait. Our Jeep Grand Cherokee sits outside the café carrying the logo'd canoe and kayak on top. Two Maliseet men at a nearby table overhear us talking to the waitress about the trip and introduce themselves.

"We couldn't help hearing about your journey. We live just up the river in Maliseet. Maliseet means 'people of the river.' We are People of the River," says the older man.

Over the next half-hour, we have one of the trip's most memorable interactions with locals. The men are brothers. The older, by what appears to be just a couple of years, is a retired engineer, and the younger is a retired teacher. They tell us about their canoe adventures on aboriginal canoe trails throughout New Brunswick. I tell them about the Northern Forest Canoe Trail between the Adirondacks and the Saint John, and how it follows ancient water trails from watershed to watershed. It's clear that we have a connection.

They share memories of the river before the major hydroelectric dams were built and inundated square miles: Beechwood in 1955 and Mactaquac in 1965. They remember a river dense with Atlantic salmon that their people fished for thousands of years. They remember when much of their natural heritage and traditional way of life was still intact. Their eyes grow sad as they reflect on what has been lost.

The men seem sad but not bitter. They don't mention that the Maliseet nation's capital of Meductic was sent to the bottom of the reservoir when the Mactaquac Dam was built. Or that the graves of their ancestors, village campsites and fertile farmland are now drowned. That would make me more than just a little bitter.

Brightening slightly, as if a tiny ray of hope has been beamed in, they tell us that the 180-foot Mactaquac Dam is failing. Its spillways are experiencing the concerning expansion of concrete, the result of using the locally quarried greywacke as the aggregate to build it. It's responsible for the alkali-aggregate reaction which causes the expansion, and has reduced the life of the spillways by forty years. There is talk of the dam's possible removal. The People of the River want to see it come down. We agree that the sixty-foot Beechwood Dam should go too, followed by restoration of the river, the fishery and the fertile valley, and generation of electric power in other ways.

Mega hydro dams have to go. If we expect to live from what the oceans are capable of giving us, we need healthy rivers. I tell them that we appreciate their aboriginal culture and the natural world. I tell them about the Native American elements of our wedding ceremony and that many times I have joined my Penobscot Nation friends for the spiritual paddle and run from Indian Island in Maine's Penobscot River to the sacred Mount Katahdin, one hundred miles upstream.

There is a bond among us; we are people with a shared compass. The younger brother asks permission to give me a blessing and wish me well. His words and his intent leave me humbled and honored. This is a moment to cherish.

It's time to get back on the water and send Nicole off to find accommodation and supplies, twenty or so miles downstream in Hartland. I wish she could stay for the rest of the trip.

At Perth-Andover, the briskly flowing river slows to a halt due to the sixty-foot high, river-wide concrete plug inserted downstream at Beechwood back in 1955. There's a bit of an upriver breeze to push against, but I'm still making good time on what amounts to a narrow, sixteen-mile-long lake.

I see the Jeep in a parking area on river left and take out above the Beechwood Dam. Nicole greets me at the water's edge and tells me that she can't find a put-in below the dam. In fact, there's no official boat access until the town of Bath, almost four and a half miles downstream.

After a lengthy portage, I'm on moving water once again. They really need an official portage trail.

Nearing day's end, my phone rings. I stop paddling and drift, pull the iPhone from my pfd pocket and answer. It's Nicole telling me where to take-out.

"You can't miss it. It's the world's longest covered bridge. This thing's almost 1,300 feet long. Take out below it on river left," she says.

Beyond a right-hand bend in the river, there's a bright red aluminum outboard boat in a calm eddy with three people fishing, likely for small-mouth bass. The end of the bridge appears on the right as I round the bend, and begins revealing its considerable length from behind a large island in the center of the river. The current picks up substantially and I realize that if I don't paddle my ass off, I'm going to be swept past Nicole, now standing at the take-out way over on the other side of the river. I'll bet she's wondering what the hell I'm doing way over here.

I spin the kayak to the left, as much as I can spin an eighteen-foot kayak with a rudder, and paddle madly toward the far shore. For almost a thousand feet, I stroke with conviction against the current and narrowly make the eddy at Nicole's feet.

"Looked as if you might've been doing another twenty miles today!" she says, chuckling.

The Ja-Sa-Le Motel is the only show in town. Fortunately, the owners are friendly and it's clean. We have dinner at a brew pub in a town downstream, and the next morning eat at the local country club, which reputedly has the best breakfast around.

I hit the river around nine and Nicole goes on reconnaissance. It's a twenty-six-mile day of bald eagles, kit foxes playing on the river bank, and whitetail deer bounding through the woods, but my take-out is still fifteen miles upstream of the lodging that awaits our arrival.

I tie the kayak onto the Jeep and slide into the passenger seat.

"You're going to love this place," Nicole says.

I've heard this before and the anticipation is keen.

Fifteen minutes later she stops the car, shifts the transmission to park, and shuts off the engine. We're sitting in front of The Big Axe Brewery and B&B. I look at her in disbelief. You've got to be kidding me. A brewery with a bed and breakfast next to the river?

Upstairs, our room overlooks the water. Waiting for us on the dinette table by the picture window are two wooden paddles, each with six holes. Dropped into each hole is a five-ounce taster of craft beer, brewed downstairs. Across the room by the entrance to the bedroom is a two person jacuzzi. Nicole has outdone herself this time, and again she's right. I love it.

Morning brings with it another separation. I'll put-in to continue on and Nicole will point the Jeep south to go home. I'm very grateful for all of the time she's been able to spend with me.

The next time she will be able to intercept me will be somewhere in Maine. First, I must paddle the rest of the Saint John and the Bay of Fundy, just to reach the Maine border. It will be many days before I see her again. I go through the launching ritual with a heavy heart. I don't want the momentum of my strokes to carry me around the corner and out of sight, but they do.

Nicole: "You're not allowed to die!"

Camping. Photo by Brian Threlkeld.

Whitewater canoeing, Saranac River, NY. Photo by Brian Threlkeld.

Bailing, Saranac River, NY. Photo by Brian Threlkeld.

Sick and freezing in the Adirondacks.

Busted by the Royal Canadian Mounted Police.

Bay of Fundy Fog.

Hauling up on Maine's remote and wild Halifax Island.

Welcome to Portland Harbor by Privateer *Lynx* and friend Fred, from Shipyard Brewing Company.

Nicole's Kittery welcome. Photo by Rob Center.

Expedition kayak and canoe. Photo by Chris Wall.

CHAPTER ELEVEN

— Lost and Found —

The river's biggest dam lies downstream and backs up the water for sixty miles, making another long, slightly wider, lake. With no current, long stretches deny the reward of making noticeable progress. With a stiff headwind, it would feel as if you were going backward. Today is calm and the timing is perfect. I step out of the kayak at Little Bear Island Campground an hour before dark. It's mostly motor homes and trailers, with a handful of tent sites on the periphery. Being preseason, there are no tenters and very few of the parked campers show any signs of life.

I land ashore, pull the kayak onto the beach at the nearest campsite, head down the waterfront driveway and up the access road to the office. I need to pay for my site and get change for the laundry. On the way, I notice a couple of recreation kayaks stored upside down for the winter under the homemade wooden deck at a trailer's entrance. Across the dirt driveway, a dock is being readied to install. It's clear they're beginning to get set up for the season. These are the first signs that at least a few people use the river.

The owner is a pleasant woman, eager to find out what I'm doing on the river this early in the season. I explain my trip and ask her about the name of the campground. She shares the backstory.

"It's named after an island, now under more than a hundred feet of water from the building of the Mactaquac Dam. The Atlantic salmon used to be so plentiful that large numbers of black bears would congregate on the island to gorge themselves. With flooding from the dam, both the salmon and the bears are gone. And with them, the island."

Nothing cheery about this story.

I tell her that I've heard that the dam might be removed and ask her about that. She confirms that removal is an option and goes on to say that they made a bad decision in 1965 when they built it, but she's not sure if removing it is a good idea, since everyone is accustomed to how things are now. She wants to hand her business down to her children and worries that removal of the dam would ruin the campground. As far as she is concerned, this would amount to another bad decision.

"It's complicated," she says.

I nod, take my quarters, and head back to the site to gather laundry.

I'm emotionally exhausted from parting with Nicole and physically exhausted from having clocked almost thirty miles today. Once the few articles of clothing are washed and dried, I make dinner and pass out in my tent.

I awake earlier than usual. Through the vestibule's no-see-um netting, the morning's first glow shows the lake as calm as it was when I went to sleep. The air barely stirs. I'll take advantage and get an early start. There are eleven miles to paddle to the Mactaquac Dam portage, and then another seventeen miles to Fredericton where I will meet Dan Carr, a paddling friend from Maine who sits on the Maine Island Trail Association board of trustees with Nicole. Dan will join me down the rest of the Saint John, the Bay of Fundy, and Maine's Bold Coast before heading home. I'm already looking forward to it.

I dress quickly, emerge from the tent, stretch my arms, and suck in a lungful of cool air rich with the fragrances of dewy grasses. Prying my eyelids apart with thumbs and fingertips, I smile at the sight of a loon paddling away from the shoreline where I left the boat. *The boat. Where the hell is the boat?* My skin turns cold and clammy. I break into a sweat. The waterline at the campsite has risen two feet overnight. The kayak was high and dry on a gravel beach and now it's gone.

"Oh no. Oh no. Oh no," is all I can say.

Barefoot, I dash to the water's edge and scan the mouth of the stream next to the site. There's no kayak. I search up and down the shoreline, straining my eyes and trying to will it into view. There's no kayak. I'm really sweating now and my stomach is churning with sour bile. *Think.*

Across the river, just visible between the limbs of shoreline trees, I spot something low to the water. I peer through branches and see that it's a yellow speck over a half mile away, reflecting the morning light. It's the kayak. I grab the paddle, pfd, and tow belt containing rope for rescue and towing. *Do I need anything else? No. Go.*

Still barefoot, I sprint to the trailer that has the kayaks beneath the deck. I grab the nearest kayak, dump the leaves and squirrel's stored nuts from it, and bolt to the shoreline, kayak in one hand, paddle in the other.

I scramble over boulders as if they weren't there, throw the boat into the water and me into the boat. In no time at all, but for what feels like an eternity, I arrive at my abandoned ship, adrift on this inland sea. As I clip the tow belt into the handle on her bow, I apologize to my kayak and promise never again to have such a lapse of concentration. Nothing like this will ever happen again. I swear.

Like many hydroelectric facilities, the reservoir behind the Mactaquac Dam is allowed to fill at night when power production is reduced due to lower electricity demand. During the day, when demand for electricity ramps up, water is passed through the generator turbines and the water level in the impoundment drops. This is the equivalent of an inland, human-made tide cycle. I knew this. I've always known this. Why did I have that lapse in thought last night? Why didn't I pull the boat way up on shore like I always do? I got away with it this time. I need to sharpen the hell up.

I was unable find any good information about portaging the 160-foot-high, concrete behemoth at Mactaquac. Seeing attendants at a park across the lake, I paddle over for some local knowledge. I ask them which side of the dam is best for portaging. They don't know, but have a sense that my best bet would be to take out on the right, then cross the roadway that goes over the top of the dam and walk the road down the left side to the Visitor's Center. They don't know if there's a place to get on the water down there. I thank them and head for the right end of the dam where a small trail takes me to the road that crosses it.

There is no shoulder on the road, and the traffic over the dam is intense. Not very appealing. I run across the road to scout out an old, gated, gravel road. It twists and winds its way down to river level where I can see there's a beach beyond a pile of boulders. Not ideal, but I'll make it work.

It takes forever. Even though I wear the pack loaded with most of my gear to lighten the load in the boat, rolling the cart over such large stones requires care. I don't want to bounce the kayak and crack the fiberglass, or ruin the cart. An hour later, I'm repacking the kayak in the blazing sun at the water's edge. It feels like summer.

The dam, with its power station across the river, is a giant, concrete monstrosity. Some may view it as a technological wonder, a beautiful thing, an achievement of humankind over nature. It's that, all right, but I've always felt that this taming of nature is not a wise thing at all. Over time, the facts bear this out. All I see is something that has damaged nature, ruined ecosystems, and robbed an indigenous people of their heritage. I understand our species' history and the need for power, but it comes at a cost and with unintended consequences, especially the major hydro projects. They need to be removed, the rivers and the ecosystems restored, and the river and ocean systems allowed to work as intended. We rely on them to feed us and will depend upon them more. As the Maliseet men said: restore the river; get power another way.

I turn my attention to what is happening on the water in front of me. It is remarkable. The surface boils with thousands of fish that have come from the ocean, their upstream migration halted by the dam. They are trapped, and unable to follow their instincts. More than two dozen bald eagles take turns tucking their wings into dives, with talons extended to snatch up easy prey. It's like shooting fish in a barrel. It's a very impressive, though sorry, show.

I'm excited. The extreme tides of the Bay of Fundy travel up the Saint John River and stop below the dam. Although still roughly ninety miles from the Bay, I'm launching into my first tidal waters, at just six feet above sea level. No more portages. Except for hauling out to eat and sleep, the kayak won't leave the water again until I am finished with PaddleQuest 1500.

Kittery, Maine, here I come.

CHAPTER TWELVE

— Friends —

I enter New Brunswick's capital city of Fredericton, and pass beneath a retired railroad bridge peppered with cyclists, joggers and families enjoying a stroll across the river on a sunny day. To minimize the carry, I check my navigation to see how close I can get to the motel where I'm meeting Dan. The kayak nudges the shore, I climb out and haul up to a grassy strip by the road. Good. I can see the Fort Nashwaak Motel sign, and halfway between it and me, is a familiar, lanky figure striding my way. It's Dan.

Dan is tall, carries himself with confidence, and has a glint in his eye that makes me wonder if he was one of those mischievous kids that some teachers love to hate. An engineer by trade, he's weaning himself off a full-time schedule to allow space for adventurous travel. Joining me for a few days figures into his new scheme. Wired like an engineer, he's detail-oriented in a way that I most certainly am not. His level of planning and note-taking leaves me dumbfounded. A whitewater kayaker and ex-raft guide, he has sea-kayaked the Maine Island Trail from west to east. He's a very experienced paddler that I definitely won't have to worry about. The guy is funny as hell and it will be a blast to spend time with him. I'm looking forward to the next several days. When he heads home, I'll be paddling alone again for the duration.

We chat while walking the block to the hotel. Dan's been following my every move on the website tracking and we've traded text messages a few times over the past weeks. It's good to finally see him. I take the kayak off its cart and we cram it into my room. This requires uncomfortable contortions and a little imagination, because it barely fits. The door just closes and I'll have to crawl over it to get to the bed, where its bow will rest on the pillow next to mine.

I quickly change and head with Dan to Cannon's Cross Pub in the motel's parking lot. The pub features beer served in mugs the size that beer mugs were meant to be. Just about requiring both hands to lift, they're called Thunder Mugs. Forty ounces? I wash a couple of burgers and an order of fries down with two of them. Dan can't believe his eyes. Later that night, we return to the bar where I order more food, more beer, and impress him once again.

Sixteen miles downstream is the town of Oromocto. There, my New Brunswick whitewater kayaking friends, Adam Tremblay and Rob Niesh, will join us in their two-person sea kayak. They have local knowledge that I need to tap into, about what lies downstream.

Depending upon the movement of the tide, the Reversing Falls of the Saint John, situated in the river's namesake city, can either be as placid as a lake or the largest, most violent Class VI rapids found anywhere. An enormous volume of water shifts back and forth every six hours. This is Adam's and Rob's backyard, where they surf giant waves in freestyle whitewater kayaks and hone their acrobatic maneuvering skills. I've asked them to join us because I'm committed to mining knowledge about places like this. It helps me to avoid being killed. After all, I did make that promise.

They know the exact phase of the tide we need and precisely the right time to be at the Falls for safe passage with loaded expedition kayaks. I'm confident they'll have us there when conditions are manageable, but my blood pressure still spikes every time I think about the Falls. I've only seen them when they had ten-foot explosion waves, recirculating holes that could eat a tour bus, and whirlpools the size of a soccer pitch.

I'm eager for breakfast and to get going. Dan seems nervous, or like he's had too much caffeine, even though we haven't had our first cup. Something's on his mind.

"John, you need a layover day," he says. "Adam tells me you've been paddling hard, racking up the miles, and you need a day off."

"But Dan, the weather forecast is great. I feel great. You just got here and it's only 16 miles to Oromocto. Why the hell do I need to rest for a day?"

"It's what Adam wants for you and we can go into town for local brews and have a relaxing day together before striking out for the Falls. He has things timed out," he says, though without much conviction.

Seems like an argument I'm destined to lose. This doesn't make any sense to me, but I capitulate. Why not accommodate the wishes of my friends who are so generously giving of their time to help me navigate this perilous part of my expedition? I suspect that something is up, some kind of conspiracy, but I go with it.

We hit the water and paddle leisurely downstream. There's no reason to hit race pace. We're not going far and, for whatever reason, tomorrow we're not going anywhere. It's killing me.

I'm told that Oromocto is the home of the largest military training ground in Canada. I hear the booming before I get there. For another fifty miles downstream, I will hear and feel the shockwaves of artillery reports piercing the air, and live munitions cratering the earth.

On a side channel to the main river, we pull up to pristine docks where a path leads to the headquarters for Eco-Logical Adventures, a paddlesports retailer that rents canoes and kayaks. The owner is a friend of Adam and has offered to let us store our boats and gear while in town. He's good-hearted, energetic, and eager to give us a ride to the Days Inn where we're staying, for two nights instead of one. I can't help being suspicious.

After we check in, Adam and Rob show up. Adam is tall, handsome, and powerfully built, with the confidence of a capable outdoorsman. Rob is also at home in the outdoors, and more than just a bit mischievous. He always looks like he's about to tell a hysterical, off-color joke. He has a truly magnetic personality, and I look forward to spending time with these guys. Add Dan into the equation and this is going to be a fine couple of days.

Forty minutes later we're being served at a brewpub in Fredericton. In no time, my huge, juicy burger and a local India Pale Ale disappear. Adam is managing a text message beneath the table, but I don't think anything of it until I attempt to flag our waitperson for another beer. Shoving his phone into his cargo pants pocket, Adam shuts me down and announces that it's time to go. Rob and Dan take their last gulps.

"We'll have a beer at the hotel bar when we get there," Adam says reassuringly.

I'm right. It's a conspiracy. They're all in on it, but nobody is showing their cards. I'm curious as hell but don't press him about what's up his sleeve.

Back at the Days Inn, the four of us walk into the bar. It's two in the afternoon, so the place is devoid of people except for the bartender, and one customer at a faraway table by a large, curtained picture window. I head over to the bar to see what, if anything, they have on draught but Adam intervenes, physically blocking my trajectory. Now, like a sheepdog, he's herding me toward the lone figure behind a newspaper sitting at the table. Lights are dim and all the curtains are drawn. It's like a clandestine meeting in a cheap spy movie. This is creepy.

I've gone far enough. I need to be able to fight or flee. Five feet away, I stop. I can see the top of a man's head. He drops his newspaper to the table and stares me in the eye. I'm paralyzed. I'm frozen. Can't move. My jaw drops. It's Rafael from Costa Rica, one of my best friends, whom I haven't seen in years. He jumps up and gives me that familiar huge Rafa hug. I feel tears in my eyes.

Adam and Dan colluded to do everything possible to slow my downstream progress so Rafa could drive to Oromocto from the airport in Quebec. The layover day is a ruse to enable the reunion. We're just staying the night after all, and will launch downstream in the morning. I'm blown away by Rafa's surprise arrival, and by everyone else conspiring to help make it happen. What outstanding friends. All of them.

Rafa and I catch up during the car ride back into Fredericton for dinner and a bit of shopping. I need replacement sunglasses that will hug my head and fit closely to my face, acting more like goggles when paddling in stiff headwinds with spray. I also need two tote bags to make it easier and quicker to shuttle gear between the kayak and campsites. Rob picks out two bags for me: one pink, one teal, both with flowers. Nice job, Rob.

Rafa is founder and president of Rios Tropicales, the preeminent whitewater rafting and eco-adventure resort company in Costa Rica. We served on two outdoor industry trade association boards of directors together. Our history goes back thirty-something years. Rafa hosted Nicole and me for our week-long honeymoon in Costa Rica, subsequent to which, we and our wives vacationed together in Peru. He's an accomplished photographer and snaps away throughout his visit. I can't believe he's here. I have to pinch myself.

We are up early for a filling, self-serve, hotel breakfast, after which we cram everything into Adam's car and Rafa's rental and head to the put-in. Adam's parents are friends of mine, too, and are big supporters of Adam. They meet us at Eco-Logical Adventures to see us off. Not long after meeting Adam, I saw a YouTube video of his dad, Richard, making the first whitewater kayak descent of the Reversing Falls. That was edgy stuff back in the day. It still is. Richard's birthday is the same as mine, February 10th. He and Adam always do an overnight sea kayaking trip on the Bay of Fundy to celebrate. My kind of people.

I'm sealing the kayak's rear hatch cover when Rafa walks over with his camera.

"For you, Amigo," he says, pulling from his jacket a clear bottle of Cacique Guaro, our favorite Costa Rican liqueur. In the images he takes, I look like I have just won the lottery.

The air is cool, but the light rain holds off until our boats are packed, and we're leaving the dock. We'll see Adam's parents in Saint John at the end of Adam's and Rob's time with us. Rafa is going back to Quebec for a little photo touring before an Adventure Travel Trade Association conference in Saguenay, Quebec. It's a bittersweet sendoff. On the dock, waving goodbye and wishing us well, are some of the best people I know. I pledge to get back down to Costa Rica, turn the boat downstream, and paddle away.

CHAPTER THIRTEEN

— River's End —

The further downstream we go, the fewer attack helicopters we see, and the concussive blasts of exploding ordnance fade. Paddling against the incoming tide's current, we pass wooden ferry boats, propelled manually by sweep oars, bow and stern. They are used to shuttle cattle across to graze the large mid-stream islands that punctuate the center of the river.

The rain stops, but it's a chilly fifty degrees with a brutal headwind jacking up two-foot whitecaps on what is now a half-mile-wide river in places. The two-person kayak is the easiest craft in which to maintain a reasonable speed in these conditions, so Adam and Rob take the lead. I paddle at the same pace, flanking them on the right. I can see the strain in Dan's reddened face. He's determined and paddling hard to stay as close behind the tandem as possible. Like a car in a Nascar race, he's seeking whatever drafting advantage he can find. The narrow ribbon of broken air and water behind the boat in front reduces his effort measurably. Even so, the battle is relentless. Dan finds himself dropping back; going it alone in the wind and waves. I look back. He's getting smaller.

Dan mentioned to me more than once that his style of paddling is to tour for a couple of hours, pull over for a pee and a snack, and then continue for a couple of more hours. Today is more my style of paddling. Hammer relentlessly until I am there, taking quick hits of water from my hydration pack on my pfd between strokes. After this, I wonder if he'll ever paddle with me again.

We halt our downstream progress so Dan can catch up, and paddle slowly to keep from being blown upriver. We can't become separated, and we can't slow down and still make the time window for paddling through the Falls. We have a total of about fifty-five miles to paddle by four o'clock tomorrow afternoon. Even with favorable conditions, it would be close. The consequences of a late arrival will be accelerating tidal flow and rapids swollen beyond reason. I don't want to think about it.

When Dan pulls up, he's clearly hoping there'll be a break. But no. Intuitively, Adam and Rob strike up a four-way conversation and we resume our paddle toward Saint John. Spirits uplifted, I stay close enough to hear the jokes being told. Dan spins yarn after yarn with his unique brand of humor; the laughing spells make it hard to paddle. Adam and Rob swap time in the spotlight with salty stories and songs. The work isn't as noticeable. We're not going fast, but we're gaining.

We milk the last glow of light from the day, and stealth camp on an island of tall grasses, mysteriously called Grassy Island. I tamp down the vegetation and pitch my tent. We make dinner and head to bed. No partying tonight. Everyone is *done* and we need to get going early.

Lying in bed, my eyes are riveted open, staring at the ceiling. Can't sleep. Adam and Rob keep telling me that the run through the Falls will be anticlimactic; that the timing is planned to make it through on flat water, before the tide shifts. I can't help thinking about the possibility of the timing being off; that we'll round the bend at the top of the gorge, the point of no return, and they'll look at me in horror, saying they were wrong, all bets are off and its every man for himself. This could be nature's way of preparing me for anything that might happen, of keeping me sharp. Right now, the only thing it's doing is keeping me from getting sleep.

We awake to another cool, gray day, but the wind treats us much more kindly. We start off paddling with the current and make good time, passing by islands, farmland, and cable ferries using huge spools to wind their way along a river-wide cable. Adam keeps checking his watch. There's an unspoken sense of urgency.

Dan's two-hourly pee stops never happen. We pull ashore on a sandy beach for a mandatory leg stretch and a quick snack that we all wish were lunch. Dan trots to the woods. We're back on the water in less than twenty minutes. I learn that we are behind, but not drastically.

A thirty-foot cabin cruiser passes in the opposite direction. Adam tells us that it has come up through the Falls at slack high tide. We're still a couple of miles away. He checks his watch.

"Well, the tide has already started to move out. She's starting to empty," he says matter-of-factly.

I feel a pit in my stomach, worrying we'll be late and it will be disastrous.

"But don't worry, boys! We're almost there!" Adam cries out.

It is like cracking the whip. We all pick up our stroke rates.

Round a bend, we meet a kayaker heading our way.

"It's Dad!" says Adam.

Richard has paddled up the falls at high slack tide, about the time the powerboat came through. He's joining us in his Inuit-style, hand-crafted, sea kayak for the downriver run through the Falls, and he's his usual bubbly self. I feel my blood pressure dropping and my breathing slow down. If he's not worried, neither am I.

We don't waste a second by eddying out above the Falls. Adam has us raft up together and continue floating with the current to discuss the rapids below. He has his game face on. Everyone, including Adam, straps on their helmets as he speaks.

"There are a few things you should know about this rapid. Geologically, it's unlike anything in the world, so I'm told. Where the gorge narrows is where two ancient continents collided. One continent is upstream of the bridge over the Falls, and the other is downstream. The shear zone, where the two collided, is under the bridge. That makes for some funky stuff going on under the water. It's 100 feet deep above the Falls and 200 feet deep below them. Between is ledge rock thirty feet beneath the surface, which makes this volume of water do some pretty unusual things. Enough tourist stuff. Let's get down to business," he says, adjusting the grip on his paddle.

I have never seen Adam look so serious. My blood pressure spikes again and won't be coming back down until this is all over.

"We're entering the Reversing Falls Gorge and the current is picking up, gaining momentum. This'll be fun, boys. As we get closer, you'll see the paper mill towering over the rapid on river right. There are islands and channels on our left. Stay away from them. There'll be a single-arch bridge spanning high above the river below the mill. We're going to run straight down a massive ramp of water below which the river moves to the right beneath the bridge. Don't go left, to the outside of that turn. There's a pretty big whirlpool over there. Ought to be the size of a couple of school buses. Once around that whirlpool, you'll see the city of Saint John. Head for it. This'll be a piece of cake. Oh, and you may find a few boils, whirlpools and waves. Enjoy the ride!" he yells, with a laugh.

With that, we separate to give each other maneuvering space. Without taking a stroke, we're already going over ten miles per hour. Game on.

I'm beyond anxious. I've been thinking about this rapid for years, ever since Adam started lobbying me to drive up here to go play boating with him. In a loaded expedition kayak, catching the rapid in full tide change would be disastrous. But I'm confident that he has brought us here at a good time. And a good time is what I'm determined to have. That's what I'm telling myself.

This place is as intimidating as hell. Gotham City meets Mad Max. On my right, the gargantuan paper mill, tall stacks belching plumes of steam, looms overhead. The enormous bulge of water beneath me feels like an angry, awakening beast. Not only do I hear it, but I feel its gurgling and hissing through the kayak and paddle. Vertical cliffs form the left bank, deflecting roiling current.

The distinct edge marking the lip of the ramp passes under my bow. Pitching over the edge, it's not what I expect. I've paddled some huge volume rivers but haven't seen anything quite like this. It's some of the funky stuff Adam was talking about.

The falling water accelerates. Everywhere, boils appear out of nowhere, lifting the boat, dropping it in unintended directions. I'm caught up in the momentum. A sudden sucking sound to my left. I snap my head to look. It's gone.

I expect to see a smooth tongue of water descending the ramp, predictably blossoming into waves and other water features at the bottom, but this is chaotic. Upwellings from the depths explode at the surface. Small rudder and paddle stroke adjustments keep me on line through boils the size of Volkswagen Beetles, cyclonic whirlpools spinning off their edges, gobbled by surging seams of more boils. Rolling standing waves appear at the end of the ramp.

I anticipate the current wanting to push me left into the notorious whirlpool at the bottom, so angle right, paddling the inside of the turn under the bridge. Back over my shoulder I see that the whirlpool could eat a couple of buses. Not a fun place to be.

It's squirrelly water, but it's manageable. Everyone has made it through. Dan and Richard are smiling. War whoops emit from the tandem behind. Near the end of the rapid, only small waves and swirling currents dissipating into the Bay of Fundy stand between me and the City of Saint John. Adam was right. This *is* fun. My blood pressure shows no sign of dropping yet. I'm elated.

The pier next to the Hilton is not intended for landing kayaks. Nonetheless, that's our plan. It's made for tall ocean-going vessels that tie up to the telephone poles driven into the sea bottom. To disembark, simply step down onto the dock. In my vessel, I'm looking straight up at where I need to go. When I stand up in the kayak, the dock's deck is at chin level. I toss gear onto the dock like I'm throwing basketball hook shots. Then, bow line clenched between my teeth, I employ climbing skills to pull myself up onto the decking. Spiderman I am not, but it works. Everyone performs their own version and luckily nobody goes for a swim. It's a team effort hauling boats and gear up onto the pier. We are unsteady on our feet, and everybody is drained. It is as comical as it is dangerous.

Richard and his wife, Adam and his wife, and Rob throw gear in cars and tie boats to racks. Dan and I carry our boats and gear to a secure room in the downstairs of the Hilton a few yards away. We all agree to meet in half an hour to go look at the Falls at full tidal flow before having dinner at a brew pub by our hotel.

The night before, when camping on Grassy Island, Dan called the hotel to confirm our reservations. I'm sure the call must have been memorable because Adam and Rob had Dan in stitches. He was laughing so hard, he could barely talk and had to apologize. He managed to tell them we were coming by water and gave them an approximate arrival time.

Still in our paddling gear, Dan and I check into the Hilton. The manager asks what we've been doing on the river. Dan tells him the tale.

"Yes, we heard you were coming," says the manager.

"I wonder what they heard," Dan says to me with a grin.

We're instant celebrities. The manager asks us what beer we'd like to have delivered to our rooms. I choose a local IPA.

As I peel off my dry suit ten minutes later, there is a knock at the door. A very polite, uniformed young man places an ice-cold bottle of beer and frosty glass on the bureau. He quickly leaves, refusing a tip. I like this place.

Hopping into two cars, we go look at the Falls. This is the spring high tide of twenty-nine feet and it's all the way out. There must be a million cubic feet per second roaring through the gorge. Adam points to twenty-foot explosion waves along the ramp we paddled down a few short hours earlier. The whirlpools are huge and dizzying to look at. Everything is exploding everywhere. It's pure chaos out there. I'm happy to be on land and thank Adam for taking us through at the right time. In its current state, the Falls are terrifying.

CHAPTER FOURTEEN

— Bay of Fundy —

The adrenaline and anxiety from running the Falls drain from my body. I sleep like a log.

In the morning, I hear the chirping of those crickets again. It's been a while since I heard them. I pry myself out of the queen-sized bed, with its high thread count sheets, plod over to the drapes, and slide them open. The room doesn't get any lighter. The icy Bay of Fundy is notorious for impenetrable pea soup fog. There it is, dark gray and wet. The condensed vapor beaded up on the window looks cold, and I know it is. Let the fun begin.

The Hilton's breakfast buffet is impressive. I gorge myself on eggs, pancakes, bacon and sausage. I stuff a banana and two apples in my pants pockets for later. Throughout our meal, Dan is studying his global positioning system to make sure he's familiar with the route and that the GPS is working properly. The dense fog is slowly lifting and the forecast is for manageable winds and no precipitation. It's a perfect day to head out on one of the most notorious pieces of ocean on the planet. We have to deal with extreme tides–today's is twenty-nine feet–but we don't have to deal with extreme weather. At least not today. Tomorrow, on the other hand, does not look good at all.

I'm excited about the ocean leg of PaddleQuest 1500, starting in the Bay of Fundy, and traversing the entire coast of Maine.

Since the first life crawled from the sea and evolved into humans, we have been irresistibly drawn back to the sea. It is a magnetic force that inspires us to float beyond the horizon into the unknown; it must be in our DNA. Ocean travel has spread humanity across the earth; not even the remotest island has been denied our footprints. We want to live next to it, play in it, and make our living on it. For me, much like flight, the sea represents absolute freedom: freedom to travel the globe, port to port, hemisphere to hemisphere; freedom from the daily hustle and being hustled; freedom from borders. If we row, sail or paddle, it's responsible, cheap travel, free of gas stops.

I keep in mind that the ocean, as alluring, romantic and beautiful as it is, has a way of indiscriminately snuffing out the hopes and dreams of seafarers. The sea bottom is littered with wrecks of sunken oil tankers, cargo ships, military vessels, cruise ships, fishing boats and pleasure craft. Bodies are entombed in the depths within every manner of transport we have devised to cross the sea's surface. Headlines constantly remind us that this is a dangerous place.

Our route will take us due west along the Fundy coast toward Maine. My goal is for us to make about thirty miles to the New River Beach Provincial Park campground. Dan is dubious. We beat on him hard for two days. I see him hoping to avoid another whipping today, but I think he knows it's inevitable. From the start, Dan has seen this stretch as a two-day endeavor, finding a place to stay in one of the few harbors along the way. It's time to lobby.

"Dan, the conditions may make this a reasonable goal for today," I say.

Dan shakes his head and laughs. "We'll have to see."

I can tell he doesn't think it's funny.

To get our kayaks back on the water, we have to put-in at the end of the cove by the hotel. It's choked with almost two feet of yellow-brown foam retched from the paper mill upstream and the sewers of Saint John. This isn't going to be pretty. At least I'll be wearing my hazmat suit.

With about 565 miles to go, I'm nearly two thirds finished. By my calculation, this last leg of the journey is the most dangerous part; the part that can end it all; the part that can make me fail to deliver on my promise to Nicole. What I have been through already has been preparation for what's to come. I have that pit in my stomach again. At the same time, I'm eager to get going, and have it be done.

Six feet above water level, we load our kayaks with gear. It takes only a half-hour, including a last pee break, but our boats are ready to float themselves on the rising tide. The prospect of entering this sea of toxic foam to make it to open water is not just gross, it's horrific. The rapid rise of the tide makes the yellow-brown foam look alive as it creeps up the sloping gravel shore. It's like a primordial ooze that might grow legs, coming ashore.

That we as a species still allow our waters to be this polluted disappoints and angers me. Yet again, we can do better.

I'm impressed with how fast the tide rises and the foam advances. I use the paddle to sweep clear a stretch of water parallel to shore in order to float the boat. I hit Play on the GoPro video camera mounted to the deck and climb in, quickly snapping my sprayskirt around the cockpit rim before scummy suds crawl in. Of all the video I shoot on this trip, this will be the nastiest.

Dan has launched. The only sign of him is the upper third of his torso floating above a fluffy cloud of yellow and brown. He's almost to open water, laughing his ass off. What else are you going to do?

Using the blades to fend off the lather as I paddle, I make my way through forty-or-so feet to open water. Upon my arrival, Dan and I splash each other's boats and gear to rid ourselves of any evidence of this alien encounter. We're careful not to get each other's faces wet. Who knows what's in it.

Saint John is a bustling industrial port and home to the Irving Oil Company. It's built for oil tankers and freighters. The port's "shores" are lined with high vertical walls of concrete and steel, where ocean-going vessels tie up to iron cleats the size of Chevy Silverados. Like the sheer cliffs of the Bay of Fundy, there's no place for a kayaker to go ashore. Several oil tankers ply the waters within the channel markers. We need to scoot out of here before something uncomfortable develops.

Hugging the long, rocky seawall connecting the mainland to the island at the mouth of the harbor, we round the corner and point west. With the port now behind, a limitless expanse of calm water lies before us, lapping a rugged shoreline to our right. The air is warm. I'm sweating. Splashing forty-degree water on my drysuit does the trick. A perfect day to crank out thirty miles. I'll bet Dan is already thinking about where we'll be stopping to pee.

Paddling from point to point along the shoreline, and crossing the mouths of bays and inlets, we draw as straight a line as possible to the west. Every hour we raft up; review navigation information and our progress; grab a snack. The tidal current is not a particular hindrance. When we meet resistance, we paddle near to the rocks and cliffs to take advantage of shoreline eddies, where we hop from one to another making swift progress.

My thoughts wander to Adam and Rob. They are animals. After two days of endurance paddling and a somewhat late evening of beer drinking, they're running a twenty-five-mile trail race this morning. I expect to hear from Adam once they've finished their race. I'll bet it wasn't easy.

The tide is now going in the right direction, and we have made only one pee stop. We eat lunch sitting in our boats. A text drops in from Adam: *I see where you are with your tracking. You're at Chance Harbour! You'll make New River Beach. Piece of cake!* I read it to Dan. He looks at the screen of his GPS, calculates the remaining mileage and looks at his watch.

"It's looking good, but we may be arriving under the cover of darkness," he says.

I'm stoked that he sees the light at the end of a tunnel that leads all the way to New River Beach. We'll have time to rest and recover tomorrow. Mother Nature isn't going to let us go anywhere.

Dan is quite the naturalist so it pays to stay close, watch and listen. He points out a pair of puffins flying toward us just five feet off the water. Only yards in front of us, they streak by. These are my first puffins. Moments later, razorbills do a flyby. My first razorbills. I'm having an unbelievable day.

By the time we're passing Dipper Harbour, our sunny day has turned gray and overcast. The atmosphere thickens. Change is in the air. We round the headland where Point Lepreau Nuclear Generating Station hums along, feeding our appetite for necessities and conveniences. Darkness begins to swallow the remaining light.

A direct line to our destination leads through a myriad of ledges draped with seaweed, exposed by the falling tide. It's seal pupping season. Moms and pups cover the rocks. I'm a hundred yards ahead of Dan, but slow so he can see the spectacle for himself. I signal to him with my hand and one of the sentinels, seeing my gesture, barks and hurls herself into the water. One by one at first, then by the tens, a hundred harbor seals vacate the ledges for the safety of the sea. The breeze shifts slightly. I smell the rancid odor of feces hanging in the air. Dark eyes look down pointed noses, keeping tabs on the intruders. Behind us, loud splashes attempt to lure us away from the herd. This is the single largest congregation of harbor seals I've ever seen.

Dan was right. Darkness is falling quickly but we're only a mile out. It's calm, with a gentle one-foot swell lifting the boats as we pass the next island, making for the shore ahead. I approach a bell buoy whose presence in the fading light evokes the conning tower of a sinking ship, rocking back and forth. With each passing swell, the deep clanging of its gong echoes eerily across the water.

We drive up on the edge of the sand beach. It's one hell of a low tide. We just about need binoculars to see dry land. It's going to be a long hike with boats and gear. I've stayed here once before when helping Adam with a whitewater kayak clinic. We camped at the group site, driving to a wonderful whitewater river nearby. I remember exactly where the pavilion is located. The tide is falling as we pull our boats well out of the water and head to the site. We find it empty. Excellent.

I walk to the park office, hoping they'll rent the group pavilion to just two kayakers. I open the screen door, walk up to the counter and address one of the rangers. As soon as I say I just arrived by kayak from Saint John, one of the rangers cocks his head.

"Are you John Connelly?" he says.

I'm taken aback, but only for a second. I remember that Adam said a paddling friend of his worked here as a ranger.

"Yes. Are you Adam's friend?" I say.

"Sure am. I'm Matt. Let's get you set up," he says.

Excellent.

The forecast was right. As we wait for our dinner over my MSR stove, the wind is blowing steadily, better than twenty-five miles per hour. The rain is horizontal and the fog bank rolls in. It's supposed to do this all day tomorrow.

The pavilion is the right choice. I've had enough of soaked tents, so set up mine right in the middle of it. Dan opts for setting up his outdoors next to the woods. At least we have a dry place to hang out together and eat. Can't fight the weather. A storm like this is the Universe saying that it's time to do laundry, so that's how we spend our layover day.

Our stay is made more comfortable by Matt, who drives us to a restaurant overlooking the Bay for dinner. Sitting at our scenic table, we can see nothing. Pea soup fog has visibility at zero-zero. Occasionally, out of the gray shroud, we see wind-whipped salt spray on the rocks below, from a sea that is now throwing eight foot waves against the shore. After dinner, our newfound ranger friend picks us up and takes us to a convenience store, where we buy snacks and beer. Today's Trail Angel.

Back at the campground, we watch surf pound the beach. Dan and I agree that if it's anything like this tomorrow when we wake up, we're going right back to sleep and will need to ask Matt about making another beer run.

In the middle of the night I wake up to pee. The storm rages on. I slide back into my sleeping bag, pull the hood over my head and close my eyes. Please let this thing pass by, is my final thought before my mind goes blank.

I wake up, and to my delight, I hear nothing. No wind whistling through tree branches, no rain pounding the side of the pavilion, no waves crashing on the beach. Crawling out of the tent, I put on Crocs. No rain gear necessary, I walk down the road to get a look at the water conditions. It's impossible to see the water. The fog is so thick it makes breathing feel almost as if I'm underwater. I walk down the beach until I can see. It's flat calm.

"Dan, let's go. Couldn't be flatter. Can't see your hand in front of your face, but the Bay is in a happy place today. We can make Lubec, Maine if we go soon," I say like a cheerleader.

The idea of paddling all the way to Lubec in a day, over 30 miles distant, doesn't phase Dan. I didn't think it would. Over our layover day, we discussed options for approaching what lies ahead. With some thirty-mile days under his belt, Dan is settling into long days with high calorie burn. He's lost a couple of pounds, looks stronger and has had a recovery day. He's raring to go.

Boats loaded, we push off from the beach into a dank, gray wall. I can just make out the end of the kayak. That's it. From here, we start to pass islands for the first time since leaving Saint John. Islands provide shelter from wind and waves, but they can also be obstacles. We'll lose them for a few miles, then pick up many of them during the final push to Lubec. Today I go home to Maine for a second and final time. I've been waiting for this.

If I were forced to navigate by chart and compass alone, I could. I'm grateful that I don't have to. The technology is unparalleled. My inReach is talking to satellites. In front of me, clipped to the deck lashings, lying atop the spray skirt, is a nine-inch screen with color chart and a triangular icon traversing my route of travel. The icon is me.

I make sure that the triangle points in the direction we want to go, and we're off. Dan and I agree to stay close enough to make out each other's boats, and be able to chat at conversation volume. Even though Dan is also using satellite navigation, we dare not allow ourselves to get separated. Both of us know our own location, but we don't know the whereabouts of each other.

As we set out, I'm acutely aware of the list of dangers that come with paddling in zero visibility; dangers that can come upon you quickly and are sometimes deadly. Little do I know, but by noon, I'll be checking all but two of these off the list, and some more than once.

In dense fog, the low, guttural thrumming of marine diesel engines increasing in volume is perhaps the most dreaded sound I've ever experienced. The hair on my neck stands up. Commercial fishing and other large powered vessels use radar to navigate in these blind conditions. Kayaks don't reflect on radar screens, so we're invisible. Back home in Maine, lobstermen refer to one kayak as a speed bump, and more than one as a rumble strip. I never find it funny when I hear that. Today we hear the menacing engines twice. The water is forty degrees, but my palms sweat.

Aquaculture salmon pens anchored in the current are not marked on charts, and there are many of them. Like the current flowing through branches of a downed tree on a whitewater river, these pens of nylon netting are efficient strainers, allowing water to pass through freely, but filtering out and capturing anything that doesn't fit between the web of threads. They are drowning machines for any kayaker that cannot find a way to avoid getting caught. Having immediate and effective back ferry skills is the key to surviving a deadly interaction. At the last second, I see one. We react quickly to avoid being swept in. I pull my rudder up and back ferry along the pen's length to get around. Not much fun.

Fishing weirs consist of poles, their ends buried in the sea bottom, with nets strung along them converging into a V. Fish, funneled into nets, are captured as they swim with the current. Abandoned weirs seldom have net remnants, but for a kayaker moving with the current through fog, these disintegrating pole barriers can create a deadly sieve at worst, and a challenging slalom course at best. I'll lose count of these today.

Current moving over and around partially covered boulders, rocks and ledges, creates unseen whitewater rapids that can be heard upon approach, usually at the last minute. These should be apparent on charts, but it can be tough to accurately identify and avoid them, especially at different stages of the tide. Interpreting on-the-fly in fog is challenging. You wouldn't want to capsize and part company with your boat. You might never see it again. The same may go for you. Today is fast water, but with rocks submerged, no real rapids.

It's early for whales in these waters. They typically arrive later. I suppose it's possible to come across one. I didn't have getting hit by a whale on my list of fog hazards. It's on there now.

Residual swells from yesterday's storm pass beneath our boats, crashing into the base of Fundy's famous high, vertical cliffs. Still invisible, the cliffs throw reflection waves back out to sea. The back and forth of wave action makes for bumpy paddling. I can see how someone could get sea sick in these conditions. The tide is against us so we stay close enough to the cliffs to use the slower eddy water along their irregular bases, but are careful not to get too close and be smashed to bits.

Ever-so-brief breaks in the fog reveal the magnificence of towering cliffs. Thanks to the wave action, I feel dizzy when craning my neck to examine the passing escarpments. Diagonal streaks of red, yellow and gray colored rock are punctuated with the bleached white guano of nesting sea birds. I feel small, insignificant. I feel alive.

At mid-day the sun takes over, trading a curtain of solid earth-bound vapor for high, fluffy cumulus clouds. We no longer need to navigate electronically like aircraft pilots flying blind through clouds. Now we can navigate by taking a heading on a point beyond and paddle to it. Stress free. Much better.

We stop in a pocket beach for lunch and to water the bushes. To our horror, there's enough plastic and trash in this remote cove to fill a bucket loader. There are discarded items from aquaculture operations and fishing boats, household items, the usual single-use plastic bottles, and indistinguishable micro-plastics pounded into tiny pieces by wave action. By sifting sand and gravel between my fingers, I can see the brightly colored fragments now part of the environment. I've heard these micro-plastics are ingested by the filter feeders and fish we eat, causing health maladies in humans.

Despite local shore cleanup efforts along the Bay of Fundy and coast of Maine, the sources of this pollution are not being adequately addressed. This detritus is being dumped into our oceans worldwide and the sea recognizes no geopolitical boundaries. I've read that experts say the sheer mass of plastics in our oceans will be greater than the mass of fish in a few short years. From what I'm witnessing, I believe it. I'm hugely disappointed in us. Once again, we can, and must, do better.

Islands are more numerous now. The sloshing of the tide creates ribbons of current that require deliberate route finding. We look for the fastest water heading in the right direction, paddle to it and go for a ride. A few yards away, I notice water streaming in the exact opposite direction. Abruptly, our magic carpet disappears, and the current punches our boats on the nose, stopping us in our tracks. For the most part though, we're finding favorable currents and making good time on what is now a stellar day. The Bay of Fundy is in a good mood.

It's called Old Sow. Just about everyone hearing about my journey down the Bay of Fundy to Maine's Bold Coast tells me to beware of it. Old Sow is the largest tidal whirlpool in the Western Hemisphere. The name apparently comes from the pig-like sucking sounds the thing makes when it really gets going. I've heard it is 250 feet in diameter; has a vortex that no kayaker wants anything to do with; and it casts off "piglets," smaller whirlpools, from its edges. It's only a mile out of our way, but I have no plans to pay Old Sow a visit.

CHAPTER FIFTEEN

— Home for the Last Time —

Our stellar day has gone gray. This time not from fog but from a steady rain with no wind. At this point in the day, this last stretch of six miles feels more like ten. Along cliffs and the mouths of coves, we travel the length of Campobello Island. Nicole and I camped here once, and on our second visit we stayed in a cabin facing toward Lubec, Maine, across the channel separating Canada and the United States. I should be paddling by the cabin any minute now.

Almost half of Campobello Island is Roosevelt Campobello International Park, Franklin Roosevelt's summer retreat, now a historic park with campground, golf course and woods. The park is run by both the United States and Canadian governments, although the island is entirely within Canada. I am excited to cross that channel. I hope the Lubec Brewing Company's tasting room is open.

I point out the cabin where Nicole and I stayed. We round a small point, and a half-mile away is Lubec, Maine, USA with its small, picturesque harbor, mostly occupied by lobster boats motionless at their moorings. Except for the outgoing tide, all is still and the rain has stopped. We need only to cross what the locals call The Narrows, and we'll be done for the day.

A phenomenal volume of water is racing through The Narrows out to sea, and six hours from now, it'll be racing back in again. It's moving fast.

Damn. Dan and I look at each other in disbelief. The harbor is suddenly gone. We're staring at a solid gray wall of fog roiling our way, determined to devour us. It does.

"That was quick. Impressive," says an invisible Dan, two boat lengths away.

With the harbor scene burned into my brain, I take a quick compass heading at our target. I estimate the speed of the outgoing tide I saw a moment ago, and adjust the heading with an up-current correction of thirty degrees. Even without navigation, this heading should put us right where we want to be. I have the inReach and iPad as backup.

For the second time today, Dan pulls out the VHF radio to make a safety announcement. He describes our position to any vessels in the area and advises that two kayakers are crossing The Narrows channel in the fog. He asks for any vessels listening to acknowledge and report their position. As with the last time, the radio is silent. We're off.

We stay close together, paddling hard to get across the channel before a fishing boat runs us over. We put some extra effort into it. Paddling hard ensures that we won't get swept past our target, through The Narrows, and out to sea. This risk provides the motivation we need to hammer across as if these are the first strokes of the day.

We cross an eddy line into slack water. A shadowy shape emerges from the fog. Her stern reads: *Fundy Morning*. It's the nearest moored lobster boat. I saw it just before the curtain came down. Another comes into focus, followed by the boat ramp. The fog lifts enough to see, at the top of the ramp, Cohill Inn and Pub where we're staying the night. Made it.

Dan has paddled extensively in this area and knows Glenn, the Cohill's manager, who is expecting us. Glenn is an accomplished expedition kayaker in his own right. Word is, he paddled from Key West, Florida to Lubec, Maine and never left. I like him already.

We've been spotted. I see Glenn walking down the hill to greet us. I'm back in the USA and back home in Maine. This time, to stay a while. We need to get to US Customs ASAP.

Glenn helps us stash our boats and gear under the deck at Cohill's. Dan and I snatch passports from dry bags and drip our way down Water Street. I notice that the brewery is open and wonder aloud if Gayle, the owner, is there.

"Apparently you're no stranger to Lubec either," says Dan.

CHAPTER SIXTEEN

— The Coast of Maine —

The US Customs building sits high above the rushing Narrows at the end of the bridge leading to Campobello Island. I've been processed here a couple of times, but never in wet paddling gear, knife affixed to a pfd loaded with radios and safety gear. We trudge in the front door, passports in hand. The customs agent behind the counter, all business and brandishing the weaponry of Homeland Security, looks us up and down.

"You're the kayakers who put out the safety call when coming across The Narrows to the harbor, aren't you?" he says.

I knew someone was listening. I knew it would be Homeland Security. We affirm.

"Where are your kayaks and your gear?" he says.

I have a sinking feeling.

"They're at Cohill's where we're staying tonight," says Dan.

No reaction.

Please don't make us go get all that stuff. The day's been long enough, I'm thinking.

"Check the forecast. You may be staying more than one night," he says, thumbing through passports, looking at his computer.

I look at Dan. He lifts an eyebrow. We thought something nasty was moving in to stay. Guess we were right.

As we answer "No" to all the questions about possessing contraband, I wait for the other shoe to drop. It doesn't, thank goodness.

"Welcome home, boys," says the agent, handing us our passports.

We're in. Don't have to go back and drag our kayaks and gear down here. Perfect. It's time to find our rooms, get changed and rehydrate. Not in that order and not with water.

The agent was right, and so is the forecast. Thunderstorms hammer the Bold Coast and we require a layover day to let things settle. Ahead is the final section Dan and I will paddle together. In Machias, he'll hop in his car to go home. Nicole will meet me with supplies for the first time since Nackawic, New Brunswick.

We watch the weather closely and hope for only one weather-bound day. It does look like the thunderstorms have moved on. Left behind are high winds, overcast skies, eight-foot ocean swells and small craft warnings. We will assess after breakfast.

With its vertical cliffs plunging into the sea, Maine's famous Bold Coast is spectacular and completely unforgiving. Like stretches of the Bay of Fundy, there are miles of exposed shoreline where ocean swells explode at the bottoms of soaring cliffs, with no inlets or coves to offer shelter if conditions worsen, or if there is a medical or equipment issue. It's wise to have favorable seas for this stretch.

After a check of weather and oceanic conditions during breakfast, we decide to go, with the understanding that, if we don't like what we see, we'll come back and wait it out. Winds currently at twenty will persist. Because they'll be coming off the land, at some point they should tamp down the ocean swell. Seas approaching eight to ten feet are expected to lessen with time. Let's go.

Glenn helps us schlep our boats and gear to the water. At the landing, it's clear the tidal current is still running strong, but it's slowing. Where the Narrows meet the North Atlantic, outgoing tide combined with the incoming ocean swells will jack up steep waves. We'll just have to get out there to see if it's manageable.

Glen waves his final goodbye from the jetty, and takes pictures of us entering the mouth of The Narrows where we experience the incoming ocean swells. I hope these aren't the last photos anyone will take of me.

The waves are so steep that the bow pitches down, surfing deep in the troughs, forcing the stern out of the water, and along with it, the rudder. Instinctively, I use a combination of directional paddle strokes and leaning the boat on its side to carve turns on wave faces, to maintain my course. Later, Dan tells me he saw two feet of my stern out of water at a time, and was impressed that I kept control.

Dan's kayak has a skeg instead of a rudder. This centerboard-like fin, three feet from the stern, is deployed by hand with a lever next to the cockpit. This helps the boat track straight, and could definitely be an advantage over a rudder in these conditions. In the prolonged cross-winds to come, the rudder will shine.

It's too much. We ferry across faces of breaking waves to the safety of a narrow cove on our right. We land and pull our boats clear of the tide. It's a little challenging. The beach is beautiful, but consists of soft-ball-sized, multi-colored, polished granite stones. We rest and consider.

Paddle back to Cohills, get rooms and drink beer for another night? Hope these conditions calm down, and just keep going? I am on the fence. I take a walk up a short trail to a field, and see we could probably camp here for the night. A check of the clock shows that it's too early to make that call. Let's see what happens.

Waiting is hard, so we decide to saddle up and probe around the corner to see how conditions are in the open ocean, without the outgoing tide. We round a rugged granite outcropping. The West Quoddy Head Lighthouse, with its red and white candy stripes and rotating beacon, stands watch over a tempestuous sea. I have a feeling that the churning bile in my stomach is here to stay for a while.

As we paddle out around the lighthouse, the waves pound the granite shore, sending spray into the sky. I see tourists gathering, pointing their fingers in our direction. They must think we're nuts and they're probably right. I hope nobody calls 911.

Swells are all of eight feet and some may reach beyond ten. One second I'm on top of the world; the next, I can only see the very top of the lighthouse. I see Dan. He's gone. I see Dan. He's gone. Repeat.

We need to talk about this.

"So, what do you think?" Dan yells from just one boat length away. There he is. Now he's gone. There he is again.

"This is freakin' huge. But it's deep and not breaking out here," I shout over the war zone to my right.

We agree that if we stay away from cliff bases and ledges, we've got this. We're good to go. Decision made, we pick up the pace. Part of me wants to go back to Cohill's, have a burger and a beer and wait for this crap to calm down. If one little thing goes wrong, I can deal with it. If two things go wrong, that's a problem. If I were alone, I'd turn around. I'm glad to have company.

What I don't say to Dan is that this is extremely intimidating. It's big water. Exposed. Unforgiving. A gale is blowing off land, requiring us to stay nearer to the cliffs than we'd like, so we don't get blown out to sea. The incoming eight-or-so-foot ocean swell is breaking against the cliffs, sending back three-to-five-foot reflection waves. When the two meet, it's very bumpy. Okay, it's more than *bumpy*. Everywhere, edges of current fold over each other unpredictably. One side of these lines helps us along; the other side stops us in our tracks and sets us back. It's a battle.

We're looking at seven miles of completely exposed paddling ahead, but have plenty of daylight to get it done. The absence of islands, coves or bays along our route leaves us naked out here. I can't help but feel somewhat vulnerable. Going ashore for any reason is not an option and there's no way to survive what's happening where these giant surges detonate into vertical granite. I simply put it out of my head, refuse to even look at it, fearing it will somehow suck me into its grip, like that terrifying hypnotic attraction that pulls you toward the void when standing close to a high, exposed edge. Can't think about it. Vanquish the demons. Have to stay focused. Relax, perfect my form, visualize the route, visualize flawless execution, visualize success. Keep a close eye on Dan. Stay together.

The crosswinds are brutal. Here's where my rudder allows me to stay on course stroking with equal effort on each side. Dan has to make strong forward sweep strokes on his left side to keep his boat on track. He's tiring from driving his bow into the wind, but we still have miles to go before our first chance for a break. It's a cove called Bailey's Mistake.

Captain Bailey, navigating by compass and chart, ran his ship aground here in the 1800s. He mistook the opening to the cove for The Narrows channel entering Lubec. I'm confident we'll have better luck on our voyage today. Red-faced, and grimacing with every stroke, Dan manages a smile when we lock eyes. The man is a wonder.

We paddle across the mouth of the cove to behind an exposed ledge. Pushed by powerful surges, I run the kayak aground in large cobble. The water recedes, the boat settles onto the stones. I yank my sprayskirt off but struggle to get out of the kayak. I have to get out before the next surge slams me and the boat into rocks. My legs are like rubber; my brain says one thing, legs do something else. The effort of getting here has left my circuitry too tired to function.

Everything about this sucks. Here comes the next surge. I straddle the kayak, waddle to the bow. I grab the bow handle as the surge lifts the boat, hurling it forward, almost pulling it out of my hand and knocking me over. I dig both boots in between softball-sized stones and hold my ground. The surge recedes, tries to tear the boat from my grip again. This is a lot harder than it needs to be, I think. Dragging the boat above the tide mark, I sit and watch. Dan is equally graceful.

There's nothing like forty-degree water with wind and no sun to drive a chill into a sweaty drysuit. We take only twenty minutes for snacks, hydration, rest, and making a plan. There's plenty of light to push on for another two or three miles to Moose Cove. If we could make it further to Bog Brook, there's a cabin we can use. I've been there before, but it's a bit too far. That ain't happening. Moose Cove, it is. In sync with the rhythm of the surge that deposited us here, we launch. This time, much less like Laurel and Hardy.

I ride the swell between ledges into protected water around a small point. There's just enough flat land to camp. I'm more emotionally exhausted than physically exhausted, but not by much. I'll sleep well tonight.

The morning brings the same cool, gray sky with half the wind we saw yesterday and a diminishing swell. We still have challenging wind and ocean conditions as we traverse the iconic towering bluffs of the Bold Coast's Cutler Reserved Lands, across bays, and finally to the sanctuary of Cross Island National Wildlife Refuge.

I'm sick of the relentless chilly wind and getting out of it is a welcome relief. The big, old, white house on Cross Island is used by the Outward Bound School for ocean programs. There's no lock on the door and visitors are invited to shelter here, as long as they leave it in good shape and close the door behind them. We still have a half day of paddling against an outgoing tide and river outflow to get to Machias. Our lunch break is less than thirty minutes. We push on.

A reporter for the regional newspaper in Washington County has been following my track online and we've exchanged texts. He's waiting for me when we arrive at the boat-landing in Machias, next to the motel where I'll be meeting Nicole in a couple of hours.

After the interview, I help Dan put his kayak on his car. I'm saddened by his departure, just as I was when saying goodbye to Brian and Ned in the Adirondacks. Dan has paddled with me since Fredericton, New Brunswick. We shared so much, endured so much, and I had the privilege of getting to know him better. I'll miss the camaraderie, having someone nearby in fog, someone to talk to, and not least, his wit. A bear hug later, he belts himself into the driver's seat.

Dan resembles a piece of burnt of toast. Not crispy around the edges, but totally burnt.

"I've never been so tired in my life," he confides, hands positioned on the wheel at ten and two.

"Are you okay to drive?"

"We'll see!" he says, then pulls out of the parking lot, pointing the car homeward.

Standing alone in my drysuit, I watch the yellow kayak, and one of my best friends, fade from view.

It's been something like ten days since I've seen Nicole. The sight of her pulling into the motel parking lot is a thrill. Helen's Restaurant, a Machias landmark with the best homemade desserts for miles, is fifty feet from our room. We catch up over scallops, local whole belly clams, and craft brews from a nice tap selection. There's much to discuss. More than anything, I just want to be in her space. In our room, I plop onto the edge of the bed and pass out before reaching horizontal. Fun date.

Instead of me retracing the four-and-a-half-mile paddle down the Machias River, Nicole drops me in the water in the harbor at Machiasport. With the vertical cliffs of the Bold Coast now behind, I plan to traverse all of Downeast Maine in two days, hopping point-to-point and island-to-island across its bays, rugged shorelines, and two of the most notorious hazards on its coast, Petite Manan Bar and Schoodic Point.

It's the typical gray, chilly and windy weather to which I've grown accustomed. I have my sights set on camping on Halifax Island between here and Jonesport. I'm completely caught off guard by what happens next.

I can barely keep it together. Saying goodbye to Nicole is as hard now as it was back on upstate New York's Racquette Lake on Day Two. I want to leave her with the image of a competent John Connelly, launching into the North Atlantic with confidence and enthusiasm; the cool dude, an inspiration. If I don't get the hell out of here right now, the image burned into her memory will be absolutely pathetic.

I quickly snap the hatches closed, give her a last hug, and climb into the boat. As I follow the shoreline out of the harbor, I glance over my shoulder just in time for a last glimpse of her standing alone at the water's edge. She disappears behind the curved shoreline of granite and timber. I feel tears wet my cheeks.

I wonder why I am such an emotional wreck. Then I realize it's about overwhelming exhaustion and the possibility of never making it home; dying out here; not making good on the promise. If ever I were aware of how tenuous the balance is between paddling safely and paddling on the edge of disaster, it is now.

I've been making responsible decisions for myself; assessing and re-assessing conditions; re-evaluating my own condition, abilities, tolerance for risk; and I've been managing accordingly. There's no getting around it; the ocean is a vast watery wilderness. Conditions change in an instant. I am a speck on the sea and my dispassionate host cares not whether I succeed or become fish food. The emotional component of this expedition is catching me off-guard, and it's powerful. Now that I've named it, I begin to get a grip on it.

The open-water crossing of Little Kennebec Bay and Englishman Bay to Halifax Island is wild. Again, the tide race opposes white-capped waves, driven by a small-craft-warning wind. Just another day of PaddleQuest 1500. I pick up the tempo, drive into the wind and waves, determined to make the island before gray turns to black.

It's huge. It's a grey seal. Unmistakable. I've heard it called the "hooked-nosed sea pig" because of the shape of its snout. Twenty yards away, its dark eyes are fixed on me. Geez, there's another one, even bigger. It's even closer. I hope there's not a third. Gray males grow to just under 900 pounds and this guy's not far off it. Females weigh half that. It could be a pair. Unmoving, except for rising and falling with the swell, they stare unblinking. They are apex predators in these waters, and I don't want to encourage a boarding party. These guys prey on harbor porpoise and other seals. Why not a lone kayaker? Four eyes are boring holes through me. Simultaneously, they slip beneath the waves. Gone, but probably not. I'm as paranoid as I've ever been. *Be uninteresting, John. Keep paddling at the same tempo; don't look them in the eyes if they surface again. Just get to shore.*

Halifax Island is as remote and wild an island as I've found. It's a wildlife sanctuary, but is on the Maine Island Trail as an overnight site. I find this ironic because there isn't a flat spot to pitch a tent on the area permitted for camping. As I pull in, it's almost dead low tide. The cobble beach is steep and it's a long way to carry the boat to where it needs to go. I scavenge for short logs to use as rollers and ease the loaded boat over rocks, above the high tide mark for the night.

This is a raw, primitive place. Sea birds circle and squawk, seals surface, take breaths and dive. Waves crash against the open ocean side of the narrow spit connecting the island's head to its body. This neck, where I camp, is clearly awash during storms. None are predicted for tonight. That works for me.

The island is named for the British ship *Halifax* that ran aground in 1775 prior to the American Revolutionary War. Reportedly, our guys rowed over from the mainland, stripped her of her guns and used them to protect the harbor at Machiasport. Not long afterward, the Revolutionary War erupted in the Battle of Machias where the British sloop HMS *Margaretta* was captured. By pure coincidence, I am camping on Halifax Island on the anniversary of this historic event. Just me, the birds and the seals. Pretty cool.

CHAPTER SEVENTEEN

— Fog, Lightning, Wind and the Whole Crazy Thing —

I go to bed in a gale, but get up to pee in the middle of the night and am struck by silence. The waves have dissipated. There's not a breath of air. What air there is, is so moisture laden as to nearly asphyxiate me. Snug in my sleeping bag, I fall asleep, optimistic about tomorrow.

It's the time, not daylight, that opens my eyes. I awake at what should be sunrise, but I need the headlamp. My elbow bumps the side of the tent, causing me to take a cold shower. Both sides of the fabric are dripping wet. The world inside is just as drenched as the world outside. Fog. Saturating fog.

The forecast looks like stagnant air for the first half of the day, then a front coming through later. Could be a doozie. Once afloat, I can see no further than the bow. A seal clears its nose, takes a deep breath, and dives not ten feet away, but I can't see it. It's time to drive the little triangle on my screen along a chain of islands, past Jonesport, across the expanses of Western and Narraguagus Bays and beyond to Corea Harbor where, hopefully, I can find a place to camp. It'll be a very big day.

Throughout the morning, I experience paddling vertigo. Three hundred and sixty degrees of gray wetness and no horizon. I know which way is up by watching water droplets fall from my paddle blade. I stare at my navigation screen, listen for lobster boat engines, and make good time connecting the way points on the chart. While I eat lunch on an island beach beyond Jonesport, the fog lifts, revealing clear blue skies, scattered cumulus clouds, and calm seas. I need to get while the getting is good, so store my snacks for easy access and launch back in. I'm at nearly race pace in just a few strokes.

Mid-afternoon, I stop on Flint Island to stretch legs and soak in the beauty of the place. I decide to take a picture. With the horizon to the west framed for a panorama shot, I'm taken aback. I pull the camera aside and squint to bring the distant scene into focus. Towering cumulonimbus clouds, complete with classic anvil tops, are dumping a torrent on the earth below. Forget the picture, I look at the radar. Thor is doing his work along a line of storms that will intersect my location soon. I look at the storm's track. If I put-in and haul ass another three-to-four miles to Bois Bubert Island, it looks like I may be able to avoid getting mowed down by the center of this storm. This is the fastest I've paddled on the trip.

Raindrops the size of marbles pepper the water around me as I jump from the kayak and pull it above Bois Bubert's high tide mark. I grab dry bags, hustle up to the woods for shelter, and watch the storm unfold in safety. Flint Island is receiving a pounding. It disappears behind a Niagra of falling water and blinding lightning strikes. Good call.

I resolved to call it a day and camp right here, but I'm now having second thoughts. The storm has passed and there's still enough daylight to make Corea Harbor as planned. Behind the storm is a twenty-mile-per-hour sustained wind with higher gusts. So what's new? Seas are now running five feet and I'm tired. But there's daylight and I can suck it up. Off I go.

I tell myself I'll poke my head around the corner and, if it's too rough, I'll return to the island and camp. It's a lie. The corner is a mile away. It will have to be horrendous for me to turn back.

It is pretty horrendous. The seas are running six feet and wind-swept spray stings my eyes. The combination of gale and building wind waves makes me think briefly about retreating, but I quickly discard the thought. After all, I'll be dealing with it rested, refueled and hydrated. I'm up for it, although anxious about Petite Manan Bar. I see it just ahead and over its entire length, as far as my eye can see, it's blowing up. The chart shows this place peppered with features to avoid: Bunker Reef, Old Bull, Inner Bar, Bar Ledge and Southwest Breaker. This is the real deal. Even on a nice day.

Fighting headwind and sharp-faced quartering waves is exhausting. Adrenaline kicks in and provides what I need. In an instant, I feel a higher level of energy, heightened awareness, and my head is clearer. Without slowing, I'm approaching the Bar with caution. It looks angry. I have to find a way through. At this lower tide, I see that it is shallow, with six-foot waves breaking over the long minefield of rocks that create the bar. There appears to be some sand mixed in, but it's mostly rocks.

Suddenly, my synapses jolt me and I'm paying attention. This place is remote. I can ill-afford a misstep. Then I see it between waves: a narrow channel between rocks, maybe five feet wide and fifty feet long, deep enough to keep the kayak floating when the surge retreats. Unfortunately, it's not straight. I have one shot or risk breaking the kayak in half. No hesitation. Full commitment. Go now.

I pick what feels like the best line between breaking surf and exposed rock. As the outflow from the last wave's flood drains out, a barnacle-covered rock the size of a fifty-five-gallon drum appears out of nowhere right in front of the bow. The rock is devoid of weed, so nothing to cushion the blow. At this speed, the enormous white barnacles will dig deep, possibly through the hull. Another adrenaline injection. Everything shifts into slow motion. The situation becomes clear to me and I jam the left rudder pedal to full deflection, lean the boat sharply all the way over on it's right side, carve a sharp left turn, and pass over the end of the hazard by an inch at the most. With the boat back on an even keel, I steer back to the right toward open water beyond the Bar. I've made it.

The adrenaline did its job, but now it's gone, and I'm as tired as I've ever been. There's no shelter and I can't let up the effort or I'll be blown backward into the Bar. I can't miss a stroke to grab a bite of fuel. I afford a lost half-stroke, putting the bite valve of the hydration pack in my mouth to gulp vital fluid. Dyer and Gouldsboro Bays pass by with their four-foot whitecaps and wind. The incessant wind.

It's been more than a thirty-mile day. Navigation says I'm almost to Corea Harbor. I tuck in behind a ledge, call Nicole to let her know where

I am, and ask her to see if any place in the harbor is open where I can get a room or camp. Last night's fog soaked everything from the inside out, and today's storm and high seas have soaked everything from the outside in. I need a place to dry out, and a good night's sleep after a day like today. If not, I'm prepared to stealth camp, soaking wet.

Relieved to be at what I think is the destination harbor, I let myself feel satisfaction and end-of-the-day tired. The phone rings. There's that sweet voice on the other end.

"Bad news, good news. Which do you want first?" she says.

"Bad news," I say, bracing myself.

"There's nothing open in Corea Harbor. Nothing at all."

"Okay, how about the good news," I say, needing to hear something positive at this point.

"I got you a room at a B&B in Prospect Harbor."

"Prospect Harbor?" I say, probably not sounding too thrilled.

"Do you have another three miles in you?" she says. I know it's a genuine question.

"I guess I have to."

"Pretty much, 'cause it doesn't sound like you're too stoked about stealth camping," she says.

I thank her with all my heart, tell her I love her and pocket the phone. Time to buck-up.

The slog up Prospect Harbor into the gale, waves breaking over the deck, wind-whipped spray peppering my face, and toiling against the outgoing tide, somehow isn't demoralizing. It doesn't make me feel defeated. It makes me feel like an animal; like I'm killing it. At least that's what I'm telling myself.

The sun has been gone for forty minutes, but it's still light enough to see the place Nicole described, just a half-mile away. It's a sprawling white house with outbuildings, across the street from a beach and field, with a white tent for functions and events. The silhouette of a man is moving quickly my way as I land.

"Hi! Are you John Connelly? I'm Ben," he calls out.

I don't have the energy to laugh about that, and have never been happier in my life to get the hell out of a kayak.

The owner of Acadia's Oceanside Meadows Inn grabs the bow handle of the kayak. I warn him it's heavy and not to strain his back. He waves me off.

"I'm good. Let's go," he says.

I grab the stern handle. I'm the one struggling. I have to use two hands. My tank is empty. Has been for a while. If I were to rap it with a knuckle, it would echo. Unsteady on my feet, sinking ankle deep in sand, I fight to keep pace with Ben. We make it inside the tent, and set the boat down. I feel like collapsing next to it.

"Your boat and gear will be safe here. Just take what you need for overnight," says my host.

Nicole has done it again.

We step inside the foyer at the inn and Ben hands me the room key. I ask him if there's a place I can hang wet gear.

"Don't worry about the room. Hang up whatever you need to dry and do what you need. That's why we have housekeeping," he says.

"Is there a place nearby where I can get dinner?"

"Everything requires a drive. You're stranded. We had a big meal tonight at home and there's plenty left over. I can bring you a plate of dinner if you'd like,"

"Really?" I say. I must look desperate.

"I'll be back in thirty minutes." He turns on his heel and disappears.

While taking my drysuit off in the shower, I reflect on its crucial role in my survival on the water. I decide to make a video, to stress the importance of dressing for the water temperature, and not for the air temperatures.

On the video, I talk about the challenge of thermoregulation when the air is warm and the water is cold. It is critically important, when a paddler becomes a swimmer, to be wearing a drysuit with enough insulation to survive prolonged exposure to cold water. It means you sweat a great deal and have to continually replace fluids. I demonstrate just how much sweat is produced, by emptying a pint of clear liquid from each drysuit bootie. It's so gross. People are going to love it.

Dressing for water temps and not the warmer air is a lesson we keep learning over and over again. The most recent example in my mind is the loss of The North Face founder, Doug Tompkins, while kayaking in Patagonia this winter. A storm came up, creating huge waves. He capsized in icy water, wasn't wearing the right gear and died from hypothermia. So tragic and unnecessary. I hope my video drives the point home. Maybe it'll save someone's life.

Ben arrives with a generous plate of food. It's gone before he leaves the building. Before he makes it to his car, I'm asleep.

Everything about the inn is first class, including the breakfast dining experience. I choose the highest calorie items on the menu. When I'm finished, Ben emerges from the kitchen.

"I can't let you go out there hungry. Let me know what else I can get you. I'll feed you until you're full," he says.

I order two more breakfasts and check the weather forecast.

This'll be a big day. I'm a bit anxious. Yesterday was a good dress rehearsal. I feel a little bolder. Maybe that's good. Maybe not. I'm reminded of the quote one of my flight instructors affixed to the instrument panel where he was forced to see it: "There are Old pilots and Bold pilots. But there are no Old, Bold pilots." I decide to call what I'm feeling, *confidence.*

Today I will round notorious Schoodic Point, the eastern annex of Acadia National Park. Its smooth granite ledges are completely exposed to ocean swell, with tidal currents colliding as they round the point. It is known to be unpredictable and even violent at times. After rounding that point, I'll head to Winter Harbor, then across the Mount Desert Narrows, which are not narrow at all, to Bar Harbor where a room at Cromwell Harbor Motel awaits. It would be nicer if conditions were flat. They're not.

I finish my third breakfast, and I look at the forecast: "Overcast with showers. Winds from the west-northwest at twenty miles per hour, gusting to thirty. Seas are running six feet." That's just great.

While Ben gives me a brief tour of the property, we chat. He has a long history as an expedition sailor. He's a kindred spirit. He invites me to return and give a talk about my expedition. He's very interesting, and I'd like to get to know him better. I reach for my credit card to pay for my meals and lodging. The man refuses to let me pay; tells me to put the card away. Another Trail Angel.

After we carry the kayak to the water, he bids me farewell and God Speed. I'm well rested, but know this is going to be one hell of a day as I strike off across Prospect Harbor toward Schoodic Peninsula.

My outdoors buddy, Rob, used to live near me in Southern Maine but has moved to Ellsworth, a half-hour or so away from Winter Harbor. We've backcountry skied in Utah; fly-fished for Atlantic salmon on New Brunswick's Miramichi; mountain biked single track; and road biked all over. Since he moved to this area, we haven't seen each other much. Today he's going to meet me in Winter Harbor for lunch. Looking forward to it.

It doesn't take long to get to Schoodic. This is a powerful and intimidating place. Concussive blasts from six-foot surf pound huge, polished, pink granite ledges; swells tower over my head; and wind gusts test my tenacity and ability to remain upright. A crowd of national park tourists line the shore pointing at me, the Lone Kayaker, mounted on his trusty craft, in the maelstrom. *He must be nuts,* they have to be saying. And who could argue?

Again, I'm battling conditions best viewed from shore, not the cockpit of a twenty-inch wide kayak. There's been a lot of this, and I'll bet there'll be more. As I round the point, I see the waves on Frenchman's Bay are huge. The crossing will be a bear in a gale. Unfortunately, it will be a headwind again. I'm already looking forward to tonight, and being off the water, beer in hand. First, I have to fight these waves and this wind, all the way to Winter Harbor for lunch with Rob.

It's the biggest bowl of scallop mac and cheese I've seen in my life. While listening to Rob talk about adventure trips he has planned, I try to wash away the stress and exhaustion with a Shipyard Export Ale.

I need to get back on the water. The outgoing tide along with huge waves and headwind will make the crossing to Bar Harbor a serious challenge, requiring extra time slugging it out. Rob helps me put the boat back in the harbor and off I go.

Halfway across the yawning Mount Desert Narrows, I see a seventy-foot, whale-watching boat hammering in my direction at what appears to be full speed. It's a twin-hulled catamaran with jet drive.

I marvel at how smoothly it speeds through substantial seas. I hope the captain can see me. I'm paddling furiously to clear the marked boating channel. I'm not going to make it, and that thing is coming a little too close for comfort.

No more than a hundred yards away, the whale-sized ship roars by leaving a wake equal to the biggest waves out here. When the wake reaches me, it's going to get violent. I'm furious. That was unnecessary. I'm sure he saw me. Why not give me a wider berth? I suppose he thinks if I'm out here in these conditions, I'd better be able to deal with it. I guess he's right.

Finally, across the Narrows, I paddle easily along on quiet water in the lee of Mount Desert Island. Tourists stroll the Shore Path behind Bar Harbor Inn, enjoying the view before dinner. Again, fingers point in my direction. This time, not because I'm suicidal. I like to think it's because they're envious of my freedom on the water as I glide along in the rapture of early evening.

CHAPTER EIGHTEEN

— Bar Harbor and Beyond —

Around a point of ledge, the harbor unfolds before me. I circle the immense, four-masted *Margaret Todd,* a tourist cruising vessel. Yachts owned by the richest of the rich rest at the docks. The whale watch catamaran, source of my earlier anxiety, is at dock along with three smaller tour boats. I pull up on the sand and gravel beach next to the town boat ramp. I'm eager to leave the kayak and shed my gear. It'll be light for another thirty minutes. By then, I plan to have the kayak on its wheels, parked outside of Geddy's Pub, while I have a frosty one. Maybe two.

I call Nicole, tell her about lunch with Rob, and that I'm safely in Bar Harbor. I'm famished.

"How long before your boat is on wheels?" she asks.

"Ten to twenty minutes."

"I'm going to get you a to-go order at Geddy's. Stop by to pick it up," she says.

She's brilliant.

A dozen people are lined up along the railing of a twenty-foot high buttress below which I'm organizing myself for the mile trek up Main Street to the motel.

"Hey, Man! Where'd you come from?" a voice calls down.

I crane my neck and see a half dozen people leaning over the railing waiting for the answer. I give them the Reader's Digest condensed version of what I'm doing.

"That's awesome! Want a beer?" the man says.

I affirm. The next thing I know, it's raining cans of Coors Light. I like Bar Harbor.

"Your to-go order isn't ready yet. Would you like to hang out at the bar?" says the host at Geddy's front door podium.

This is going according to plan. The only one in a drysuit and pfd, I'm once again the focus of interest. The lady on the nearest barstool buys me a beer. I tell her, and five-or-so others leaning in, about my expedition.

"Double bacon cheeseburger, fries, pepperoni pizza, large salad to go?" someone calls out.

"That's me."

Nicole has done it again.

Under the street lamps, in my paddling gear, and pulling a kayak up Main Street, I must present a spectacle. Couples and small groups congregate along the route. There must be fifty people snapping cell phone pictures, but not a soul talks to me, or asks me what I'm doing. How odd. I park outside a convenience store, and scurry in for a six-pack to go. Dinner is now complete. After eating, I drift into blissful unconsciousness. What a day.

The day's first light has just shown itself. I fire up my camp stove in the room, make coffee and oatmeal, check the forecast, and pack up. The skies should clear and the wind greatly diminish.

Wheeling the kayak back toward the put-in beach at the boat ramp, I have only four blocks left to go when one of my wheels explodes. Not repairable. So close, yet so far away. Damn.

Quickly, I move everything to the curb, out of the way of cars or pedestrians. Who can help? There are several outdoors retailers, kayak and bike rentals in town. I end up connecting with Acadia Kayak and Bike. Katie, the manager, is willing to help.

"We don't have kayak carts, but I think I have something that will work," she says. "I'll be there in ten minutes."

A young woman with a bicycle kiddie trailer for twins is heading my way. This has to be Katie. We exchange the briefest of pleasantries, pick up the loaded kayak and balance it on the trailer. Me at the bow, Katie at the stern, we guide the contraption down the sidewalk to the water's edge and lift the boat off, placing it in the sand. I can't thank her enough. She scurries back to work. Yet another Angel.

Again, the forecast is wrong. The winds are still stiff, and shifted more out of the north. This gives me big, following wind waves and opposing incoming ocean swells, making for a bumpy ride along the vertical cliffs of Acadia National Park. Combined with fishing vessel wakes from a third direction, this morning's paddle has my full attention.

Passing the tall Otter Cliffs, I round the leeward end of the island. My nerves are a bit frayed from chaotic water and the occasional breaking waves washing the deck. I reach calm water and watch Sand Beach pass by on my right, tourists on shore pointing the way. There's Thunder Hole. I'm ticking off all of the park's featured attractions nearly as fast as I would if driving the Park Loop road.

I need to get to the Little Notch Bakery and Cafe in Southwest Harbor for a bit of publicity for my sponsor, Shipyard Brewing Company. I'm already looking forward to the break. I land at Dysart's Great Harbor Marina and walk the short distance to the shop. The owner is enthusiastic about photo ops for social media, makes me a killer chicken sandwich, and pours me my first Island Time IPA. It's a new session beer from Shipyard. I'm impressed. I take a couple to stash in the boat for the campsite tonight.

I leave Southwest Harbor, and notice that not only is the sun ablaze, but the wind has dropped out completely. As I paddle among brand new Hinkley yachts at their moorings across from their birthplace on my right, I can't help but marvel at the woodworking craftsmanship and their sleek lines. Elegant craft designed specifically for these waters. The smallest is worth much more than my house.

Skirting ledges rolled over gently by small ocean swells, I pass Bass Harbor Lighthouse. I think back a couple of years to when I made a video, set nearby, about how to brew Adventurous Joe Coffee with an Aero Press. That was a calm day, too. At the foot of the lighthouse, a dozen people watch the sun sink to the horizon.

Forty-five minutes before sunset, I arrive at the head of Bass Harbor, landing on Sawyer Island, a MITA campsite. I quickly make camp and eat. Night begins with a loon serenade, and as the fiery ball drops below silhouettes of pine, the sky bursts into reds, yellows and blues. The next moment, stars take over and the moon dances on the harbor. It's Island Time.

Caffeine, breakfast, recharge hydration pack, organize snacks, get outta here, in that order. The harbor is still, and salt air fills my nostrils. The kayak is half loaded by the time the sun peeks over the pines. Today's forecast, clear with a light breeze, suggests the best weather I've seen on the ocean so far. I'm guardedly optimistic; they've been wrong more often than not. Today's crossings are big ones, but with calm seas and little wind, I should be able to rack up the miles.

I thread my way between lobster boats, motionless at their moorings, while seagulls circle and squawk. I exit Bass Harbor, with Thurston's Lobster Company on my right. Seafood, beer and a killer location, it's a pity there isn't time to stop. I like it there. Next time.

I round the point marking the southwest corner of Mount Desert Island, and Blue Hill Bay is smooth. Not quite a reflecting pool, but as quiet as the ocean can be. Time to kick into high gear.

Terns and gulls over Pond Island welcome my passing, circling near, giving me a good looking over. Jericho Bay, through the islands of Merchants Row, remains just as smooth. My mouth is watering. I can't stop thinking about the double cheeseburgers at Old Quarry Ocean Adventures and Campground in Stonington. I hope Captain Bill is there. We go back a long way, to when I started what was perhaps Maine's first guided sea kayaking company in '80/'81. Great guy.

Sure enough, Captain Bill is working on his tour boat as I pull up to the dock.

"Hey, Captain Bill!" I call out. His face scrunches, trying to figure out who is calling him by name.

"Is that John Connelly?" he says.

I love it.

Two big, fat cheeseburgers annihilated, I slide back into the kayak. My sights are set on the crossing to Vinalhaven, the large island in the mouth of Penobscot Bay. One last wave to Captain Bill and I pick a line between the dozen or so islands of Merchants Row, and go. Across from town, the captain of a lobster boat steaming back to Stonington's wharf, nods and waves. It's good to be seen.

As I approach Crotch Island, tall cranes rise above the tree line, and I'm jolted by the deafening sound of steel into rock. What has to be one of the world's largest jackhammers pounds away at granite bedrock to be shipped to the highest bidder. Known for its high quality, Maine granite has long been quarried for the construction of iconic structures and monuments across the country, and is prized for kitchen countertops. I don't think the countertops are sustainably produced. Crotch is slowly being removed from the face of the earth.

Thankfully, it's quitting time. The hammer's rage is replaced by peaceful, gurgling water draining from shoreline rocks, and the chattering gulls overhead. Before me is the six-or-so-mile crossing to Vinalhaven. There is considerable chop and the tide is pulling out to sea. I note the sun, now in a losing battle with the overcast, is getting lower to the horizon. Seeing no approaching vessels, I leave the shelter of the last exposed ledge and call upon Bill's cheeseburgers to shoot me across.

I haven't gone a quarter mile when, out of nowhere, a large, deep water, lobstering vessel appears on my left. Steaming at full throttle, its wide, high, pointed bow is all I can see. I'm sure that's all the captain can see, too, when looking forward. It is unlikely that he can see me. These guys also rely on radar, and I'm invisible to him. It's coming right at me and closing fast. I think of the lobstermen's speed bump joke. Still not funny.

Less than a hundred yards away is an exposed rock, behind which I can shelter. Rocks show up on radar. I'll be safe if I can get behind this one. I'm at race pace again, laser-beam focused on the rock, watching the white hull grow exponentially bigger in the corner of my eye. Now I can read the registration numbers. They have lobster boat races. I'll bet this one's a contender.

Almost there. No longer a head-on, he's definitely going to pass behind me. I glide past the rock and thank it. The kayak and I rise and fall as the lobster boat's wake passes beneath. Neither captain nor crew turn their heads in my direction on the drive-by. Still invisible. That's as close as I've come to being a speed bump. Who needs this kind of anxiety?

West of Vinalhaven is rugged Hurricane Island. Once a granite quarry like many Maine islands, it has been home to the Hurricane Island Maine Outward Bound School for years. These days, the Hurricane Island Foundation operates science and outdoor education programs for youth. They do great work out here. I'm fortunate to have friends on the board of directors and advisors, so I call in a favor and score a place to spend the night.

With darkness only half an hour away, I'm relieved to be pulling up to the docks. An energetic young woman rushes to welcome me.

"You must be John Connelly," she says. "Welcome to Hurricane Island."

She takes me to a place by the main building, where I hang my wet paddling clothes, then up the hill to my cabin.

"We saved you plenty of food for dinner. We thought you'd be hungry after all that!" she says. She's right.

The hospitality couldn't be more impressive. The thirty-something miles from Bass Harbor on Mount Desert Island to Hurricane Island has been quite a day. Captain Bill's cheeseburgers notwithstanding, I am famished.

After a quick change, I grab my headlamp and bolt to the mess hall. Staff gather around to learn about my expedition and ask questions. I try not to embarrass myself by wolfing down the sampling of leftovers prepared by the Foundation's chef. It's delicious.

Another night in a coma; I don't remember sleeping. The day's forecast is for stellar conditions once again and I feel rested. I stage my gear on the cabin's deck, as a bald eagle soars overhead. It's going to be a great day.

With the backpack slung over my shoulder, I head to the mess hall for a buffet-style all-you-can-eat breakfast. I stack my plate high.

At the dock, staff are loading two white-hulled pulling boats with kids in their early teens wearing orange lifejackets. The small, ocean going vessels are rugged but elegant. Propelled by eight rowers, and two masts with sails raised in wind, these vessels are designed as much to teach as to ply the seas. With their positions in boats sorted out, the kids listen anxiously to directions and any hints as to how their day may go.

Trepidation is etched into adolescent faces that represent a diversity of origin I'm sure is unique to this Maine island. For them, today will be a learning experience like no other.

I lean over the edge of the dock to snap on one more hatch cover, and I'll be ready to push off. Today is a roughly ten-mile crossing of the remainder of Penobscot Bay to Muscle Ridge then on to Tenants Harbor, Port Clyde and beyond. Another big day. A beauty.

One of the staffers I saw at dinner and breakfast clomps his way across the wooden dock, a bumper sticker in one hand and an apple in the other. This bright-eyed young man with sandy brown hair and kind smile leans over me as I snap closed the hatch lid.

"Would you like an apple?" he says.

"Sure. Thanks." I take it and put it in the dry bag with my snacks.

"I'd like to give you something; some things," he says, kneeling next to me as I sit crosslegged.

He presses a nickel-sized, polished stone the color of midnight into my palm. He tells me it's from the shore of a distant Penobscot Bay island.

"The stones there are magical. Rub it to keep it polished and it will bring you luck," he says.

I'm struck by the kindness in his eyes, and humbled by his gesture and intentions.

"I'd also like to give you this," he says, passing me the Hurricane-Island.net sticker.

"I'd like you to have the message I wrote on the back," he adds.

I flip it over. In blue pen is written:

Do not live in the past in anger.
Do not live in the future in fear.
Live in the present in awareness.

I stand up, tell him I'm grateful, shake his hand, and give him a hug. I'm buoyed up, knowing that kids, like those boarding the pulling boats, are being mentored by young men and women like this.

CHAPTER NINETEEN

— Plastic, Whales and More Cheeseburgers —

As I round the south end of Hurricane Island, there is not a breath of wind and a flat calm sea. I can't believe we're spinning through space at 67,000 miles per hour. Maybe it's all a sham. Maybe the moon landing was faked after all.

I point the bow toward the next piece of *terra firma*, Muscle Ridge, a cluster of granite islands ten miles away. They appear as a tiny irregularity on the horizon. To their left, only the featureless curvature of a watery planet.

Twenty miles, two Clif Bars, three turkey jerky sticks and a quart of water later, I'm making good time and the ocean is still calm.

"Hey John! Hey John Connelly!" I hear. To my right there's a man running from a small house to the shore.

"John, it's me, Scott!" he yells across the water.

I jam the rudder over and stroke to shore.

I bob just off the rocks, and we chat briefly. Scott invites me to The Dip Net Restaurant around the corner in Port Clyde for a late lunch. I happily accept.

"Go past the lighthouse, the one in *Forest Gump*, and I'll meet you at the first dock you see," he says.

Now retired, Scott was part of the outdoors product development group at L.L.Bean; another colleague I've run into along the way.

We hop into his pickup for a short ride into town. I sit down to an order of fried whole-belly clams and a Shipyard Export.

"I've been watching the blue tracking line on your website. I knew you were coming, so I kept an eye out, hoping to derail your progress for a few minutes," he says. I'm glad he did.

Scott manages his family's shorefront rental properties. He's a captain and maintains a few lobster traps for grocery and beer money. Finally untethered from the corporate pressure cooker, he's doing well and it's great to see him.

Across the buoyed ferry boat lane to Monhegan Island, I continue into Muscongus Bay. The ocean is calm, with a slow, hypnotic pulse of one-foot swell gently lapping the shore. Six miles later, I pull into the campsite on the west side of Black Island. Low-angle light of a day nearly spent, forms waves of gleaming flashes that dance across the smooth faces of dark granite blocks.

I was introduced to this site by my paddling friend, Chris, this past winter. Chris teaches outdoor education courses at Camden High School and is a sea kayaking guide. He officiated at the wedding of our New Brunswick friend, Adam, at which I was best man. With wavy, shoulder-length, blond hair, Chris resembles Sammy Hagar. That may not be a coincidence, since he plays in a Van Halen tribute band on weekends. Chris and I paddled out here last winter and he told me that this is his favorite campsite in the Bay, and it became mine. A beautiful spot.

This time, I'm horrified. The shores of the island are covered in wrecked fishing gear and trash. Within fifty yards of what should be pristine shoreline, there are a dozen mangled lobster traps, a couple of fifty-gallon plastic barrels, countless yards of plastic rope, styrofoam coffee cups, Bic lighters, empty Five-Hour Energy bottles, and fragments of micro-plastics coloring the gravel beneath the kayak. Black is one of the Maine Island Trail Association sites. I take a couple of pictures and email them to the MITA office.

I read in *The Washington Post* that the World Economic Forum published a report saying: "If we keep producing (and failing to properly dispose of) plastics at predicted rates, plastics in the ocean will outweigh fish, pound for pound, in 2050." Every piece of plastic we have ever produced is still here, unless it has been incinerated, and many parts of the world use the ocean to dump their trash and garbage, thinking it just goes away. It doesn't. It's still legal to dump trash overboard in international waters offshore. Really? We've got to cut that out. Not only because of the aesthetic, which is horrific, but also because our ecosystems are damaged, sea animals are harmed, and micro- and nano-plastics are finding their way into the fish we eat. If we aren't going to right the ship for them, how about we do it for ourselves? A wave of disappointment comes over me, once again.

However, there is some hope. Within a few days, the season's first MITA island cleanup of this area will take place. The island will be spotless when the MITA crew leave with their skiffs piled high with debris, and it will be maintained throughout the boating season. Still remaining, however, will be the micro-plastics, forever embedded in the beach and sea bottom, now part of the ecosystem. After I finish this expedition, I'll have a few days of rest, then I am scheduled as one of MITA's volunteer monitor skippers, driving skiffs island-to-island, and maintaining sites. Skippers are also enthusiastic ambassadors, spreading the word about Leave-No-Trace outdoor ethics and enjoying the water trail responsibly.

MITA does excellent, and important, work. However, cleaning up here and there, at sites and on islands along the Trail, isn't solving the global problem. We have to figure out how to cut off this scourge at its source. It is vital that we up our game.

I crawl from my shelter and wander to the shoreline to pump the bilge. The cloudless sunrise is as spectacular as last night's sunset. Trundling back through the rocks, I exchange waves with a lobsterman hauling traps from the depths, a few yards off the granite ledges where my tent sits empty beneath scraggly pine. The early morning light is electric, making colors come alive; nature's version of high definition. The air is still. Another calm day.

After thirty minutes or so of paddling on glass, I clear all islands and near the mouth of Muscongus Bay, approaching Pemaquid Point.

Fifty yards in front of the boat, twenty feet of black back arcs to the surface then disappears. Close behind, there is a blast of air through a vent, then a geyser of water blows ten feet into the air, and produces glittering rainbows in the morning sun. The second back, with its short dorsal fin, passes in front of me at just twenty-five yards. They're getting closer. Surfacing together, they take breaths and veer away. I feel the hair stand up on the back of my neck. The shot of adrenaline is intoxicating. I stop paddling and am mesmerized watching their departure. Hearing loud, sharp gasps of breath on my left, I whip my head around.

Not one, not two, not three, but at least a half-dozen harbor porpoise follow the minke whales. The pod passes within fifteen feet of me. I'm slack-jawed. This is awe-inspiring. I feel like I'm in a National Geographic episode. What magnificent animals. What a gift to see them so near, from my kayak. I'm absorbed in the moment, taking it all in. Never thought to grab the camera. Hands down, the best wildlife moment of the trip.

As I round Pemaquid Point, lighthouse visitors point in my direction. They're probably appreciating the beauty of a kayak on the ocean, not pointing in disbelief and wondering if they should call 911. What a difference a couple of days make.

Crossing the mouths of the Damariscotta River and Linekin Bay, I turn into Boothbay Harbor. There's a sixty-foot Hatteras motor yacht steaming into the harbor. I sprint like I haven't paddled a stroke all day, intercept the giant water plow and fall in behind. Nobody on board notices that I'm surfing their three-foot wake, getting a fun free ride into the harbor. The captain reduces speed and the wake disappears. I tuck into the swirling eddy water behind the stern and, just like in Nascar, I draft the ship all the way to the mooring field deep within the harbor. There's the Tug Boat Inn a few strokes away. Beer. Change. Meet Nicole. In that order.

All I have to do is tie the kayak to their dock, grab my overnight stuff, walk by the hot tub we'll visit when night falls, and climb the stairs to our room. Later, my daughter, Elizabeth, will be meeting us for a Father's Day dinner. With plates piled high with seafood, and possibly lobster straight off the boat, there is no question that I am living large. Tonight.

It is a joy to dine with these two. An outside table by the water, set for three, is perfect. Last night was a granite ledge outcropping by the water set for one. That was perfect, too. We haven't seen Elizabeth in some time, so there's a lot of catching up to do. She's a physician's assistant at an oncology practice in Augusta. I'm so impressed that she thrives in that environment. I couldn't do it. I'm proud of her. This is a great Father's Day.

Saying goodbye the next morning, Nicole says she'll see me later. I'm not sure what that means, but pass it off. As I get closer to home and closer to the end, she'll be able to intercept me more often. This time, saying goodbye as I leave her standing on the dock has less gravity.

What a day. I'm faced with another forecast for no wind and seas running maybe a foot. I've got to take advantage of the good weather because it isn't going to last. I decide to pass under the bridge connecting Boothbay and Southport Island, to enter the Sheepscot River. This puts me along shorelines and minimizes open ocean paddling. Below the bridge on the left bank is a familiar form. It's Nicole. She's taking pictures. I'm stoked. We get to say goodbye again.

The area around the mouth of the Kennebec River is famous for deadly, turbulent waters, especially when the outgoing tide is in full throat, and I have to pay full attention. The channel runs fast and is deep enough to accommodate Navy battleships built upriver at Bath Iron Works. It's a wonder they can run those things through such a narrow passage. I'm floating in a recirculating eddy the size of two football fields, created by an oblong island on river left. The eddy current cycles upstream, hits the downstream flow and reverses direction in a counterclockwise slow spin. Between me and the other side of the channel are standing waves four and five feet high. Some are breaking. I need to have a snack and think about this. My phone rings. It's Nicole.

"Want a cold beer?" she says.

"What?"

"If you want a cold beer and a crabmeat sandwich, they, and your wife, are waiting on a blanket at Popham Beach State Park," she says.

"You've got to be kidding me."

"Nope. Come and get it!" With that, she hangs up.

Popham is a quarter-mile away, on the other side of the Kennebec's frothy mouth. Forget the snack. I take a sip of water from the hydration pack and drop down in the eddy. The waves are smaller the further down the eddy I go. Where they're running a foot and a half high, I cross the eddy line with speed, at a forty-five-degree angle, and ferry across the wave train to the other side, catching some nice surfs on pulsating waves along the way. Heading toward the state park beach, I skip across a shallow sandbar into calm water. As I approach the beach, that special, familiar figure stands by the water's edge. I don't waste time getting there.

I pull the kayak high on the beach, then plop myself on the blanket with a Monkey Fist IPA in one hand, a crab roll in the other, and Nicole sitting next to me. I'm in a drysuit and pfd. She's in a bathing suit. We get lots of stares. No doubt, some are jealous. Of me.

Nicole tells me that our friends have a place for us to stay tonight on Bailey's Island in Casco Bay and they'd like to have dinner with us at Cook's Lobster and Ale House. That sounds great to me, but hastens my departure. I've already paddled over ten miles and that means I have more than that to make Bailey's by dark. There's a six-mile open water crossing involved. As long as conditions stay favorable, I can make it. If they deteriorate enough, I'll have to take a sheltered route. That would add a day. Chasing the last bite with the last sip, I launch.

"See you later," she says.

I shake my head. Amazing.

Leaving Popham and Small Point behind, I enter familiar waters. Eastern Casco Bay and Western Casco Bay are my regular runs as a monitor skipper for MITA. Before me is a long crossing. There are two-foot swells and a steady wind against my left ear at five miles per hour. I take a beeline heading to Bailey's Island and hit a brisk tempo.

I nudge up on the crescent beach behind Cook's Lobster, and Nicole greets me once again. Our friends, David and Jane, show up just as I finish trading my drysuit and wet clothes for restaurant-ready attire, next to the Jeep. Within minutes I'm sitting in front of a pint of IPA and a cheeseburger the size of a trash can lid.

CHAPTER TWENTY

— Most Accidents Happen Within a Mile of Home —

After dinner, I trade texts with friend and sponsor, Fred, from Shipyard Brewing Company, and learn that the tall ship, Privateer *Lynx*, will be sailing into Portland tomorrow. The captain would like to fire a cannon blast to welcome me to port.

"If you could be here at five o'clock pm tomorrow, that'd be perfect," says Fred.

"No problem," I reply, tempting fate.

Up with the birds, Nicole and I have coffee, watching the morning brighten, relaxing in one of the nicest houses around. Our friends found us a beauty. It's a shame not to linger, but I have to bolt. The forecast is for an offshore, twenty-five miles per hour sustained wind that will, once again, be a headwind. Inshore, the wind is predicted to be somewhat less, but not by much. Seas are running four to seven feet.

Our friend, David, with whom we had dinner and who hooked us up with the awesome overnight digs, wants to paddle with me as I depart. He is paddling an open-cockpit, recreational kayak and the waves are beginning to jack up. After a couple of hundred yards, he turns back. I poke out around the tip of the peninsula, and take the full brunt of wind and waves. It's all of twenty-five miles per hour and these are definitely seven-foot waves. To make Portland by five, I'm going to have to leave it all on the field. Something tells me I'll be paying for days of idyllic conditions.

The seas are biggest for the two-mile crossing between Haskell and Bates Islands. There's a barely perceptible respite on the leeward side of Eagle Island, midpoint in the crossing. This was polar explorer Admiral Peary's home, now a museum. Once to Bates, I can pretty much island hop all the way to Portland.

Halfway across Western Casco Bay, approaching Bangs Island, a twenty-foot Mako roars in my direction, water spraying away from its bow, and almost over it in cresting waves. It looks like it's going to t-bone me. At the last second, it backs off the plane, settles down, and pulls alongside. I can't believe my eyes. It's my good friends, Ned and Brian, who canoed with me in the Adirondacks. Accompanied by their two beautiful women, they are a welcome sight.

"We watched your track online and thought we'd run out here to say "Hi" and see if you'd like something to eat, and a beer," says Ned.

I couldn't be more appreciative, but I explain that I need to be in Portland by five. I apologize for not being able to hang out, but I do grab a quick snack. Ned asks me which tall ship is expecting me. Privateer *Lynx*, I tell him.

"I used to crew on that ship. She was built in Rockport, Maine and is a replica of a vessel by the same name from 1812. She's an educational vessel owned by a nonprofit," he explains.

Ned is one of those guys who has done just about everything, especially if it's nautical.

For the next twenty minutes, Ned positions the powerboat upwind of me creating a wind block, making it easier to paddle while we all chat. They sense that I need to stop talking and paddle hard to make it in time, so they say goodbye, wish me well, and head off in a hail of noise and spray. More extraordinary friends.

The outgoing tide and wind, between Great Chebeague and Long Islands, have created a seventy-five-yard-wide swath of four- and five-foot breaking waves. I hug the eddies along Chebeague, then catch an exhilarating surf to the far side across five-foot waves with small piles of foam cascading down their faces. There's something about surfing waves which stand over my head, while jetting across the oncoming water, that makes me giddy. It's going to take a while to wipe this smile off my face.

A quick check of the time. If I maintain this pace, I'll be half-an-hour late; fashionably late. In the distance, I can see her. Two tall masts rising high above boats at the marina. That's my destination.

When I am a few yards from the ship, the cannon discharges. A plume of blue-black smoke tumbles across the water and quickly dissolves in the gale. Crew and guests lining the ship's railing let out a cheer. I can see Fred. Nicole is here, too. What a welcome to Portland Harbor.

I pull up to the dock where the *Lynx* is tied.

"What does a guy have to do to get a beer around here?" I call out to Fred.

Before I can scramble out of the boat, Fred has a Shipyard Export Ale in my hand. It's a good day.

I check with the *Lynx*'s captain.

"What's the wind blowing, Captain?"

"The offshore wind came inshore. It's blowing a steady twenty-five with higher gusts."

"I thought paddling in was a lot of work," I say, and polish off the bottle.

The Atlantic is getting rowdier. The next three nights are spent at The Inn at Peaks Island, compliments of Shipyard Brewing Company which owns it. I have to wait out thunderstorms and high seas. Nicole is staying with me and commuting to work by ferry, sampling life as a Casco Bay island resident for a couple of days.

There's a break in the weather and I'm ready for it. One o'clock in the afternoon will see a severe cold front running through with embedded thunderstorms and high winds. Until then, winds are calm and the ocean is once again in a good mood, with two- to three-foot swells. I pack and launch at seven o'clock in the morning.

Nicole is catching the seven o'clock ferry. I sit in the kayak, secure the spray skirt, and wave to her as she drags her rolling luggage down the pier to board. Using my paddle like a pole, I give a forceful push to start sliding the kayak into the water from the sand and gravel beach. I hear a crunching sound, and the boat stops its forward slide. *That's going to leave a mark.*

It didn't sound or feel all that significant. I lift my knees up under the deck, and hunch over to extend my arms as far as possible, pushing hard to lift the boat gently off the beach. I inch forward. Now I'm floating. It's a spectacular morning. With this early start, I should be able to make the thirty miles to Kennebunkport before the front gets cranked up.

Why is the boat listing to the left? I'm confused. I haven't experienced this before. Down-weighting my right butt cheek to level the boat, I instantly feel coolness against the backs of thighs and calves. There's only one thing that can be. I rip off the sprayskirt. To my horror, I'm already a third full of seawater.

I do a one-eighty, and paddle like a madman back to the beach. Nicole sees what is going on and stops on the gangway to the ferry. I ram ashore, jump out, grab the bilge pump, insert it into the cockpit and spew a four-foot stream of water from the boat with each stroke. Nicole and I lock eyes. In seconds, she's on the beach with her overnight bag. The ferry blows its horn and pulls away.

Rocking the boat onto its side reveals a hole the size of a silver dollar. It has to be from sliding over an unseen sharp rock buried in the beach. It sure did leave a mark. Time for a fiberglass repair. My plans are going all to hell.

They say that most accidents happen within a mile of home. There might be something to that.

Ironically, I'm at the closest point to home that I'll be on this expedition, a distance of about four miles across the bay, straight up the Presumpscot River.

The next few hours are spent drying the inside and outside of the boat, applying fiberglass patches, allowing three hours for curing, and then Gorilla Taping it all for good measure. I load the kayak and am ready to push off, much more carefully than ever. Nicole boards the one o'clock ferry in darkening skies, and light rain showers. My timing couldn't be worse.

CHAPTER TWENTY-ONE

— What Doesn't Kill You Makes You Stronger —

My calculus is that I have enough daylight to make Kennebunkport if I put in a strenuous effort. If I round the corner between Peaks and Cushing Islands and don't like what I see, I'll simply turn around and stay another night. If there is lightning along the route, I won't go at all.

A check of radar-in-motion shows lightning above and below the route of travel. My path is clear of electricity. Current ocean conditions indicate two-foot waves with wind already at twelve miles per hour. The radar provides precise information; the conditions report I take with a grain of salt. With a quick gulp of water from the hydration pack, I pick up the tempo and head out to take a look.

Around the corner, I see that the reported conditions are wrong. Seas are already at four-to-six feet with winds closer to twenty miles per hour. I move to the exposed south end of the island, and have to contend with the swell criss-crossing the reflection waves off the rocks of Cushing. In a third direction, the Eagle Island Tours boat puts up a three-foot wake as it steams by at fifty yards. Again, tourists point at the kayaker, whose boat is now completely awash with breaking waves; only a torso with paddle sticking out of the Atlantic.

How can I escape this mess if I need to? From my vantage point, the coastline from Portland Headlight to Two Lights looks like six miles of granite being pummeled by big waves. Later, I will learn that kayakers call this the Southern Bold Coast. It appears that I am committed to ten miles of exposed paddling. Time to reassess.

There is lightning to the north and south; at least a six-foot ocean swell with contrary four-foot wind swells; twenty to twenty-five mile per hour sustained winds, gusting higher; and horizontal rain. Visibility is a little better than ten miles and there's virtually no vessel traffic. I see two lobster boats doing the right thing and returning to port. Radar shows that the cold front's leading edge is severe but narrow; only a couple of miles wide. This should be the worst of it. Should I turn around? I'm handling it, but it's intense. Am I having fun? I can't let any little thing go wrong. Feels familiar.

I've been in conditions like this three times already on this trip. I'm not gripped and feel oddly composed; weight centered, not tippy, fluid hips letting the boat move under me; relaxed torso rotating fully with each stroke; no death grip on the paddle. I'm on edge, ready for anything. Heightened awareness is around twelve on a ten scale. So yes, I'm having fun. Onward.

On the other side of Cape Elizabeth, I find relatively sheltered water between Crescent Beach and Richmond Island. The tide is falling, so I can see the breakwater of jagged rock between the mainland and Richmond Island growing with each passing swell. If I can't find a place to squeak through the breakwater, I have to go around the outside of Richmond, another mile or so. I've had enough of the outside exposure for now.

I probe the end of the breakwater next to the island, and find a slot between boulders wide enough for the boat. As it lightly scrapes the sandy bottom, I think of Gorilla Tape and wince. There's just enough water. I'm through.

The rain and gusts have stopped, the wind is dying down considerably, and the sun is out. The cold front was potentially deadly, but I was within my comfort zone and now it's gone. Ten chaotic miles down, about twenty easier miles to go. Or so I think.

At the midpoint of the ten miles of open water between Richmond Island and Biddeford Pool are a pair of islands: Bluff and Stratton. That's a good place for another snack, and to take a deep breath and keep going. This is the fastest, most direct route across the mouth of Saco Bay. I have a plan.

By the time I clear the point of Prouts Neck, I'm fully exposed to the damnable wind. It has shifted. Now out of the west northwest at fifteen to twenty miles per hour, it's a direct crosswind trying to blow me out to sea. Could this get any more fun?

If I have any difficulties, or if something unforeseen hinders my ability to paddle at full strength, I'm heading for Portugal. I have to scrap the idea of a direct route, crossing open water. Forced to paddle the inside of Saco Bay, nearer to Old Orchard Beach and Saco, miles are added, but it's a safer decision. I make my peace with it and paddle into the wind, waves washing over the bow, water shedding from the deck before hitting me in the chest.

Finally, around the point at Biddeford Pool, I now feel like I'm racing the sun. It's lower on the horizon than it should be at this point, if I'm to make Kennebunkport by dark. Nicole and our friend Fred from Shipyard will be waiting at The Colony Hotel where Nicole and I are spending the night. I don't want anyone to worry. I'm glad I don't have to take time to call or text. They can see my tracking line. They'll know what's up.

I skip around the small granite islands known as Goose Rocks. Wind is less of an issue now. It's dying out. Cape Porpoise is in sight. I hope to pass between the islands of the Cape, which provide shelter from the ocean swell. With enough water, it's a direct line. If I pop out the other side of them, I will have less than three miles to go before landing on the beach in front of The Colony Hotel, where I'm sure a cold beer awaits. This was my plan before a morning of boat repair.

I heard, and the chart confirms, that the islands of Cape Porpoise are high and dry at lower tides. This is a lower tide and they're right. Between each island is nothing but muddy clam flats sitting well above my head. I'll be paddling on the outside. There are reefs and breaking six footers. The day will be even longer than I hoped.

I am grateful for no wind. The swell, although sizable, gently picks me up and sets me down. There's a kindness about it. I feel like the ocean somehow acknowledges my toil and is cutting me some slack to end the day. The sea appears black, and the sky almost black. The white water of breaking waves is easily spotted, as if illuminated with phosphorescence. Brighter with every turn, the beam of Goat Island Lighthouse's rotating beacon is no longer being absorbed into daylight. Islands have morphed into black featureless cutouts.

The Secret Service is watching me. I know they are. It's almost completely dark as I round the tip of Walker's Point, President Bush's Maine home. The lights are on, and I don't see security personnel, but I'm sure there are plenty. Not a good spot to pull over and take a leak.

Around two more points and I'm staring at the historic grand hotel with saltwater pool, two bars and two restaurants, lighted rooms and walkways reflecting on the backs of gentle swells. I hope they're still serving. Silhouettes on the beach, Nicole and Fred stand waving me in.

The stress of almost sinking; burning precious time undergoing repair; paddling in the extreme conditions of a potentially deadly storm; hours of battling persistent high winds to crank out thirty miles before dark, add up to a pretty big day. Once again, I am happy to have this day over.

A can of Island Time IPA hits my hand as I drag the kayak onto the beach. Fred has the priorities straight.

"Tell me what I can get you to eat. I want to catch the kitchen before it closes. Nicole will show you to your room. I'll meet you at the restaurant by the pool," he says.

I give him my wish list, and he's off.

Two double cheeseburgers, a mountain of fries and three IPAs later, I am dead to the world in our room. Nicole inserts her ear plugs.

The forecast for the next three days is for no wind, clear skies and seventy degrees. If only they are right. What an awesome way to finish PaddleQuest 1500 that would be. Taking our coffees for a stroll by the saltwater pool validates the weather report, for this morning anyway.

I say my goodbyes to Nicole, Fred and John, our gracious host and general manager of The Colony, and put in on glassy water. Forget hugging the shoreline, this is an open water day and I'm beelining it for Nubble Lighthouse, twelve or so miles distant. Beyond the lighthouse lies another six miles of ocean to where I will rest my head. Tomorrow will be the seventy-fifth, and final, day of PaddleQuest 1500.

It will be a short three miles to the finale event at the southern end of the Maine Island Trail on Fishing Island in Kittery, Maine, across the yawning Piscataqua River from Portsmouth, New Hampshire. I'm going to soak up every last moment. Tomorrow will be bittersweet but today is magical: blue sky, blue water, seagulls, mild swell, and light breeze. As good as it gets.

Floating in the eddy by the lighthouse boat landing, I down a snack. The lighthouse keeper makes his way down steep steps to the landing. He's eager to strike up a conversation.

"Where you heading?" he asks.

He slides his dinghy into the water.

"The more interesting question may be: 'Where did I come from?'" I say, and tell him my story.

He's both intrigued and suitably impressed, and asks me if I have a website. He commits it to memory and rows across the gut to the mainland.

Six more miles to today's destination, Brave Boat Harbor. I love that name. Makes me think about this kayak. I'll join Nicole for a night at our friends' house on Cutts Island. It'll be good to see Melissa and David. She's a lot of fun and David has a reputation as a brilliant homegrown chef. They have room for us in their guest house. I'm looking forward to it.

I plaster another layer of sunscreen on my face. The sun is the most intense it has been since I started. The third week of June is a whole lot nicer than the second week of April.

I slow down as I pass the mouth of the York River. For the past couple of months, I've pretty much hammered my way through the day to rack up the miles. Today is different. It's early and I don't have much further to go. I need to savor this last full day. The last day of paddling alone. The last day of this long and most grand adventure.

I'll be sorry when it's over, but I won't be sad to stop. The North Atlantic is a dangerous place. It tested me, and at times seemed to taunt me. It's being kind to me on my last couple of days. I'm ready for some stress reduction.

Actually, if I'm honest, I'll be glad when it's over.

CHAPTER TWENTY-TWO

— All Good Things —

I'm anxious and up early. Again, Nicole has worked her magic. June 24th, the last day of PaddleQuest 1500, has been planned down to the minute. A flotilla will meet me as I approach the end point of the expedition. A Maine Island Trail Association skiff will shuttle folks out to the finale on Fishing Island. Friends, family, sponsors and supporters will be there to celebrate my safe return and the completion of this first-ever expedition. There'll be craft beer and local steamed clams. I need to be on time. David helps me shuttle gear to the harbor where I left the kayak cabled to a tree, then takes off to get freshly dug clams for today's event. What great friends.

Alone, I don my drysuit and load the kayak like I have every other day. Nothing is different, even though the sun is blazing, the ocean is like a reflecting pool, and I only have three easy miles to go. I'm treating this like every other day, not taking anything for granted. What if some freakish thing happens and I am not dressed properly, end up in the water and become hypothermic just before the finish line? How lame would that be? Not the media event any of us have in mind. I'm seeing this through to the last stroke. No mistakes.

I pause a moment, before sliding into the kayak, to take stock of what has happened over the past seventy-four days; how I have changed, how I have not changed, and what I have learned. The experience has been enriching and challenging in so many ways: the *Are you John Connelly?* phenomenon; Trail Angels; horrendous, deadly, spectacular, peaceful, and calm weather; violent lakes and deadly seas; my exceptional and supportive wife and friends; moose, seals and whales, loons calling in the night, perched eagles watching me pass by; manure, wheels and car parts in the river, trash and plastic on beaches; sunsets and moonrises, driving rain and blowing snow; waking to frozen paddling gear, sweating in my dry suit, suffering intestinal bugs, losing my boat, almost sinking; towering pines, towering cliffs, towering waves. Moments that terrified me and forced me to reach deep. Moments that brought me unspeakable joy.

All these things combine to give me an appreciation for the raw beauty and raw power of nature, the abundance and quality of our natural resources, and drives home for me that we need to be less careless, less arrogant and less greedy. We must tread more lightly and nurture our host planet, upon whose bounty we depend.

The experience reinforces my appreciation of the vital importance of good, clear decision making, and constant reassessment of the risks and my tolerance for them, given quickly changing circumstances and conditions.

I never once thought of reaching for the ibuprofen bottle and I feel strong, as if I could do this forever. At the beginning, I weighed in at 183 pounds and now weigh 186, but have dropped a pants size and feel great. This expedition has been a gift. More than anything, I am grateful for the opportunity.

A mile from the mouth of the Piscataqua River, I see a familiar figure approaching, blades shedding arcs of sparkling water in bright sunshine. I'd know that lanky stroke anywhere. It's Dan intercepting me for the paddle in. Not only did he spend several days in New Brunswick and Maine's Bold Coast with me, but he's here to see this thing finished. Great friend.

Careful not to decapitate each other with our paddles, we exchange hugs. Seeing Dan touches me. We've been through a lot. Unforgettable times.

Unfortunately, he has bad news to share.

"You know that cold front that blew through three days ago, when you left Peaks Island for Kennebunkport?"

"Of course. How could I forget?"

"Well, it turned out to be a deadly storm. There was a party of three sea kayakers, a guide and two guests off the Sally Islands near Corea Harbor that day. Did you hear about this?"

"No, go on."

"The storm blew up the seas, they all capsized, and two died. One was the guide. The wife of the other man who died, miraculously was rescued. She was hypothermic, but she made it."

"Is there more information?"

"It's early in the investigation, but word has it that they were not dressed for the cold water. It was a warm and sunny morning when they put in. When everything went to hell in a hand basket, all three capsized. Not dressed for it. The cold water got them. I'm sure more details will emerge, but that's what we know now."

"What a tragedy. Sounds like it never should have happened. How ironic that, not four miles from where it happened, I made a video about dressing for cold water and not warm air. So sad."

Dan shifts gears.

"Okay, that's all the bad news. You've almost made it without dying, John, and you had plenty of opportunities. Well done. I can tell Nicole is psyched!"

"I am too, Dan, but it ain't over until it's over. I'm not there yet."

We round Horn Island into the mouth of the River. I see a flotilla of a dozen or so rowing shells, sea kayaks, canoes and the Maine Island Trail Association skiff loaded with reporters.

Pinch me. Is this really happening?

There are television cameras and reporters with voice recorders and note pads. For the first time, it hits me that maybe what I've been doing is newsworthy after all. It's not just me *willing* it to be so. How cool. I'll say a few words and then it's time for a real party. I realize that Nicole made all of this happen.

No current, no wind, unlimited sunshine. It's perfect. Floating next to the boat of reporters, I answer a barrage of questions.

"What do you like better, canoe or kayak?"

"What was the scariest part of the trip?"

"Are you sorry it's over?"

"Do you want to keep going?"

"To answer that last question: if the expedition had been reversed, finishing on the Northern Forest Canoe Trail's beautiful rivers, lakes and streams, it would be tough to stop. But the watery wilderness of the North Atlantic, while spectacularly beautiful, can be a spooky and deadly place. I made it here unscathed, and I'm happy to be done. So, the answer is no."

"What's your next big adventure?"

I pause and look at Nicole.

"It won't be solo. Next September I'm rowing on a sixteen-day commercial whitewater rafting trip down the Colorado River through the Grand Canyon. When Nicole and I were dating, I promised I'd show her the Canyon by raft. It's time to make good on that promise. Then, I'm thinking PaddleQuest 3000 with Nicole. Somewhere tropical."

Glancing in her direction, I see eyes burning a hole through my head. I can tell I have some lobbying to do.

I paddle with a flotilla of friends to Fishing Island. The end of my 1500-mile saga is surreal. I can't believe all these people showed up to see me over the finish line, on a weekday no less. It's a cliché, but I'm 'feeling the love.' I'm humbled. The MITA boat drops the reporters off at the dock, returns to the island, and lands softly on the beach.

The greeting is beyond my expectations. A large group of smiling people crowd the island's shoreline. While I'm still in my boat, Nicole throws herself on me and Fred hands me a beer. It's twenty minutes before I can get out of my wet gear. I emerge from behind the island's only bush in dry clothes, and a bottle of Veuve Clicquot Brut is shoved in my hand. The steamed clams are ready. Standing in front of the PaddleQuest 1500 banner, with all of my wonderful sponsors' logos proudly displayed, I say a few words while bright sunshine bathes us all, and sea birds wheel overhead. The words are too few and don't say enough. It took a team of phenomenal people to make this thing happen.

I just did the paddling.

About the Author

John Connelly co-authored river guide book, *Appalachian Whitewater: The Northern States.* A contributing author for *National Geographic Adventure Online, Cooking Light Magazine* and in-flight magazines, he has had articles published about outdoor adventures, the health and wellness benefits of paddling, and the direct relationship between adventures in the wild and resource conservation and stewardship.

John has been in the adventure tourism industry since the 1970s and has founded whitewater rafting operations in the northeastern and mid-Atlantic states of the US and in Europe, including sea kayaking operations in Maine, North Carolina and Florida. As an athlete member of the United States Canoe and Kayak Team, John competed in whitewater world cup and world championships. After a decade of developing outdoor retailer LLBean, Inc.'s outdoor adventure, education and experiential retail business, he has been consulting in the outdoors space, primarily in the areas of safety, risk management, customer experience and operations. John volunteers as a monitor skipper, stewarding island sites, for the Maine Island Trail Association.

John has been a keynote speaker at conventions and events providing entertaining insights about his expeditions and the lessons learned. John is working on his next book and resides in Yarmouth, Maine with his incredible wife, Nicole. Check out www.paddlequest1500.com for information about his books, speaking engagements and getting in touch with John.

WERNER

Made in the USA
Columbia, SC
06 February 2023

11843422R00100